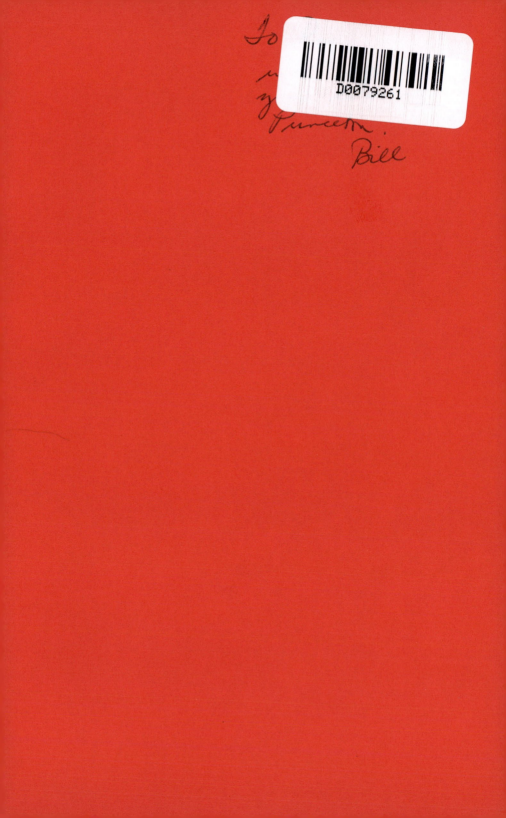

To
m
y
Princeton.
Bill

From Servitude to Freedom

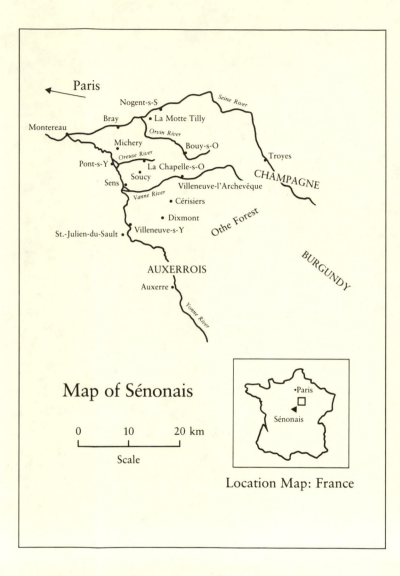

Map of Sénonais

```
0        10        20 km
|___|___|___|
      Scale
```

Location Map: France

FROM SERVITUDE TO FREEDOM ⟲

Manumission in the Sénonais in the Thirteenth Century

WILLIAM CHESTER JORDAN

uⲣⲣ *University of Pennsylvania Press · Philadelphia*

THE MIDDLE AGES
a series edited by
EDWARD PETERS
Henry Charles Lea Professor
of Medieval History
University of Pennsylvania

Designed by Adrianne Onderdonk Dudden

Copyright © 1986 by the University of Pennsylvania Press
All Rights Reserved

Library of Congress Cataloging-in-Publication Data

Jordan, William C., 1948–
  From servitude to freedom.

  (The Middle Ages)
  Bibliography: p.
  Includes index.
    1. Slavery—France—Yonne—Emancipation—History.
  2. Saint-Pierre-le-Vif (Monastery : Sens, France)—
  History.   3. Yonne (France)—History.   I. Title.
  II. Series.
  HT1179.Y66J67   1986   306'.362'094441   85-22722
  ISBN 0-8122-8006-7 (alk. paper)

Printed in the United States of America

Contents

Preface

This study began as an investigation into the effect of manumission on a large group of people owned by a thirteenth-century French monastery. Over time and thanks to the helpful criticisms of a number of readers, I have expanded it to regional proportions. It will be clear, however, that much of the original focus has survived in the illustrative case study. It has survived because I believe it adds vividness to the general arguments and conclusions expressed in other sections of the study.

Among the most helpful critics were David Abraham, John Baldwin, Anthony Grafton, Edward Peters, Leonard Rosenband, Kevin Ryan, and Joseph Strayer. I wish to acknowledge and thank the staffs of the Municipal Libraries of Auxerre and Sens and of the Departmental Archives of the Aube (Troyes), Indre (Châteauroux), Nièvre (Nevers), Seine-et-Marne (Melun), Vienne (Poitiers), and chiefly of the Yonne (Auxerre) where I spent considerable time consulting manuscripts during four separate stays in France. I must acknowledge, too, the Committee on Research in the Humanities and Social Sciences of Princeton University

vii

and the Department of History of Princeton for financial support and released time to carry out the study.

Throughout the book the usual scholarly conventions have been employed. Familiar names of medieval figures are in the traditional form: so, Philip Augustus rather than Philippe Auguste. Other names are rendered in French wherever possible, though the notes provide the interested reader with the original forms of the names. Whenever multiple references are furnished, citations to primary material precede those to secondary literature. Coinage presents a special problem for readers familiar with English medieval history. The pounds, shillings, and pennies referred to in this study are French currency and monies of account. In the thirteenth century, English sterling was worth about four times more than French money: one English pound was the equivalent of four pounds *parisis* and of five pounds *tournois*, the two principal French monies.

Finally, I wish to dedicate this book to Professor Joseph Reese Strayer, one of the great medievalists of all time, my teacher, my colleague, and my friend.

PART ONE

Status and Manumission

⟅⟆ 1
Historiography and Sources

The Sénonais, a region in France roughly coterminous with the modern *département* of the Yonne, lies approximately eighty to one hundred sixty kilometers southeast of Paris. It is bounded to the west by the Yonne River and to the north by the Seine. In the Middle Ages, the great forest of the Othe, larger and more impenetrable than it is now, formed the eastern frontier. Unevenly settled and underexploited, the forest remained throughout the Middle Ages a favored haunt of reclusive wise men and wolves, especially as population pressures in the twelfth century drove them from the Sénonais proper. There is not and has never been any easily defined boundary of the Sénonais southward; the region simply shades into the somewhat more rugged Auxerrois and Burgundy.[1]

The regional landscape is gentle. The extreme north, toward the confluence of the two delimiting rivers, is a Champagne-like plain; in the south there are low rolling hills. Watercourses frequently interrupt the terrain without ever really breaking it. Most of these are easily bridged tributaries of the Seine or the Yonne.[2] They include the Vanne, the Oreuse, and the Orvin, picturesque tiny rivers that in the Middle Ages provided the livelihood and attached their names to a number of small and sometimes still seductively beautiful villages: Bouy-sur-Orvin, La Chapelle-sur-Oreuse, Pont-sur-Vanne, Saint-Martin-sur-Oreuse. Together with the settlements on the major rivers—Marolles, Nogent, Noyen, Passy, and Villiers on the Seine, and Misy, Pont, and Villeneuve-le-Roi on the Yonne—one gets an initial impression that the skein of waterways knit together the people of the Sénonais in the Middle Ages. The existence in the medieval period of an extensive and integrated network of tolls and the frequent instances in the surviving records of conventions regarding community fishing rights underscore the importance of the hydrography.[3]

As its name implies, the regional capital of the Sénonais was Sens. This was no arbitrary appellation, for the rhythm of life in the Middle Ages was largely determined by things that happened in Sens, the only urban center that can be classified as a major town. Some indication of the difference between the size of Sens and the villages in its rural hinterland in the thirteenth century is provided by a royal fiscal account detailing benevolent gifts or aids given to the king of France for a crusade in 1248. Nothing certain is known about the method of assessment—and for any number of reasons the relevance of the size of the gifts to a precise index of population may be doubted—but it is clear that Sens was of a different order of magnitude as an inhabited center. Leaving aside Villeneuve-le-Roi (the modern Villeneuve-sur-Yonne), which may have been assessed higher as the king's personal property, the contribution of Sens for the royal crusade was twenty times more than that of its closest rival in the Sénonais (Table 1.1).[4]

Without a doubt the unique demographic situation of Sens gave a sense of regional community to the whole Sénonais. The needs of the city imposed or required (cause and effect are impossible to distinguish) a relatively high level of economic integration of the whole area. The local hydrography advanced integration; an extensive network of roads complemented the rivers. Among these, old Roman roads provided the basic outline for land trans-

Table 1.1   Contributions of Sénonais Communities to the Royal
Benevolence of 1247–48 for the Crusade

Community	Contribution (*Pounds* parisis)
Sens	2,000
Pont-sur-Vanne	100
Dixmont	40
Pont (-sur-Yonne)	40
Champigny-sur-Yonne	8
Saint-Clément	40
Gron	40
Gisy-les-Nobles	20
Lailly	10
La Chapelle-sur-Oreuse	4
Grange-le-Bocage	10
Villeneuve-le-Roi	2,400

SOURCE: M. Bouquet et al., eds., *Recueil des historiens des Gaules et de la France*,
24 vols. (1738–1904), 21:273–74.

port and communication. Travelers in the thirteenth century,
for instance, still used one Roman route from Sens northeast to
Bray-sur-Seine and another, in the direction of Paris, along a
northwestern arc from Sens through Villeneuve-la-Guyard, Villemanoche, Pont-sur-Yonne, and Montereau. A third ran southward from Sens to Villeneuve-sur-Yonne. Less significant roads,
most of putative Roman origin and all radiating out from Sens,
put the metropole into contact with a host of towns: Pont-
sur-Vanne, Molinons, Villeneuve-l'Archevêque, Mâlay, Paroy,
Noe, Vaumort, Gron, Michery, Plessis-Saint-Jean, Cerisiers, and
Arces.[5]

One can doubt whether local scholars who have reconstructed
many of these patterns are entirely correct to attribute their origins to the Romans. Even so, the general picture seems a fair one.
The centrality of Sens and the unity implicit in this persistent

network (for if it was Roman, it persisted until the Renaissance) coupled with an elaborate set of backroads of medieval origin that recent work has described, for example, around the village of Michery assured from a logistical standpoint that almost every settlement fitted neatly into and benefited from the transportation and communication networks of the regional economy.[6]

Besides topography and the network of roads, political factors advanced regional integration in the Middle Ages. Customary law derived its distinctive features from the charter of Sens, with many villages adapting that charter for their needs but without significantly distorting it.[7] The charter of Sens was a variant of the customs of Lorris which a large part of the remainder of Sénonais villages adopted directly.[8] The result was that the law of the Sénonais varied little from settlement to settlement.[9] The law promulgated in these charters was enforced under the more or less watchful eye of the French crown, for Sens had given its allegiance to the king of France in 1055, and from the late twelfth century onward the Sénonais had been administered by a royal official known as the *bailli*.[10] The only potential rival or threat to the crown's preeminence in the Sénonais or to the integrity of Sénonais law was the count of Champagne and the customs of his county,[11] but as we shall see the thirteenth century was a period of reversals for the lords of Champagne.

Beginning with a series of disastrous political confrontations with the crown, the Champenois leadership retreated more and more, early abandoning, as it were, its interests in the Sénonais.[12] I am not speaking here of the Champenois nobility in general—the Traînel family, for example, retained enormous prestige and influence in the Sénonais[13]—but of the counts. In 1228 the count and the king agreed to arrest the flow of servile population between their domains, that is, along the western frontier of the Sénonais.[14] Later, the count alienated to the crown his residual rights in Sénonais towns such as Bray-sur-Seine and Montereau where he had earlier lost his predominant influence.[15] The royal and comital lords formally delimited the border between their domains in 1270, thus reinforcing the crown's unique political ascendancy in the Sénonais.[16] A few jurisdictional squabbles occasionally erupted until, in 1284, the marriage of the heir to the French throne to the countess of Champagne removed any further rivalry between the two authorities. This *rattachement* became final in the next year when the prince acceded as Philip IV. But the Sénonais as a distinctive unit was firmly established by that date, and it retained its administrative integrity.[17]

The regional cohesion was reinforced by the ecclesiastical organization of the archdiocese of Sens. To be sure, the Sénonais made no neat single ecclesiastical district; it was simply part of the much larger archidiaconate of Sens.[18] Nonetheless, the subset of archpresbyteries (later rural deaneries) that comprised the Sénonais took its form from the network of major (Roman) roads. Consequently, like the roads, the subset of archpresbyteries centered on and took what common sensibilities they enjoyed implicitly from Sens. It was virtually certain that a churchman's economic interests, founded on the reality of topography and logistics, would also be congruent geographically with the area assigned for his ecclesiastical duties. And for synods and discipline he would be called always to the archepiscopal see of Sens.[19]

What was true of the secular clergy was true of the regular clergy as well. Although lordship in the Sénonais was extremely fragmented[20] so that an abbey like the famous Saint-Pierre-le-Vif of Sens might own one right in a village in which the ties of dependency of the villagers and their property to many other ecclesiastical and lay lords were intensely varied, few ecclesiastical institutions that possessed property within the Sénonais possessed very much outside it. This was true even with Saint-Pierre-le-Vif itself, the oldest abbey, and with the cathedral chapter of Sens, which might be presumed to have had much wider proprietary interests mirroring the size of the archdiocese. But in fact, with a few exceptions, Saint-Pierre and the cathedral chapter were Sénonais institutions in the strictest meaning of the phrase.[21]

A study of the archives of the other establishments reveals the same pattern—with even fewer exceptions. The Benedictine abbey of Saint-Remy of Sens had most of its properties, men, women, and rents around Paroy, Soucy, Villemanoche, and similar villages scattered about the Sénonais.[22] The abbeys of Sainte-Colombe of Sens, Saint-Jean of Sens, Valuisant, La Pommeraye (Notre-Dame de Sens), Escharlis, and Dilo; the convent of the Dominicans of Sens and of the hospitals of the city; and the nunnery of La Cour-Notre-Dame de Michery had their interests confined roughly to the same general district.[23] In fine, the Sénonais was a *pays*—a *pagus* in the proper sense of that word—a perception attested from late Antiquity[24] and still felt with some pride even today.[25]

This book, using the Sénonais region as its environment of study, is a history of the manumission of men and women in the thirteenth century, a period during which many lay and ecclesiastical seigneurs throughout France decided to free their dependents or to remove vile customs that debased their status. The Sénonais was a land of widespread *servitus* and of other lesser but still heavy forms of debasing disabilities on the rural and urban population; yet, Sénonais lords, like their counterparts elsewhere in northern France, undertook to lift these disabilities from their dependents in the course of the thirteenth century.[26] The reasons they did so are varied and complex. The attitudes and hopes of those freed are difficult to get at. And the effects of the manumissions are, even after much research, still controversial. But all of these issues are important and deserve examination.

That such a study should be attempted at all, given the obstacles, owes much to the inspiration provided by recent research on estate management in the Middle Ages, on the rhythm of popular discontent, and on the nature of urban experiences.[27] Work on estate management in thirteenth-century England, for example, has been particularly important in shaping my approach to ecclesiastical lordship. For it has been shown time and again, going back to the seminal achievements of Michael Postan, that the organization and management of estates and the quality of lordship profoundly intruded upon the routines of daily life of agricultural tenants and paid laborers. It has not always been possible to generalize from these studies to all kinds of lordship because the data have survived in abundance mostly for monastic estates: Barbara Harvey's study of Westminster Abbey, S. F. Hockey's discussion of Quarr Abbey and its estates, Edmund King's investigation of Peterborough Abbey, and Sandra Raban's careful analysis of the estates of Thorney and Crowland are a few of the more recent products of this tradition. The research of Christopher Dyer on the estates of the bishopric of Worcester and that of Barbara English on the lands of the lay lords of Holderness are two of the infrequent successful examples where this sort of research has been attempted for nonmonastic estates.

Another type of study that raises different issues and exploits different sources is conveniently labeled the "Toronto School" after the distinguished Toronto professor Ambrose Raftis. The works produced in this tradition aim at recovering the "community of the vill," a phrase that serves as the title of the book by Edward Britton, one of the scholars associated with the Toronto School approach. By focusing on those parts of England where strong series of manorial court records have survived, an effort is made rigorously to identify individuals over time, their conveyancing of property, their marriages and lineages. The innovative methods whereby linkages are made have been useful in the present study even though surrogates for manorial court records, which are absent, have had to be employed.

Yet, it is not the methodical construction of linkages that is most interesting in the work of the Toronto School. It is the results: the evidence points insistently to the tightness of local communities and to multiple ties that bound individual to individual. Even avowed critics of the school, like Zvi Razi, have been deeply affected by this insight, as in his *Life, Marriage and Death in a Medieval Parish*. At its best the Toronto School produces vivid pictures of peasant interdependency and the equilibrium of daily life, as in

Edwin DeWindt's *Land and People in Holywell-cum-Needingworth.* At its worst it tends (1) to ignore social conflict by overstressing the stabilizing influence of ties among individuals and (2) to de-emphasize conflicts between lords and tenants by insisting upon the "reasonableness" of demands laid on peasants, without considering how or why those demands came to be reasonable.[28]

The value of the two types of study thus far described rests in the particular questions they raise and in the comparisons they offer. Geographically more relevant, however, are two sorts of research that have been going on apace. The first again focuses on rural life, and the researchers are constituted by the intellectual descendants, increasingly the critical descendants of Marc Bloch. From Georges Duby, through Françoise Lehoux, Jean Richard, Robert Fossier, to Yves Sassier, these scholars and a troop of others have written regional histories, usually though not exclusively agrarian in emphasis, until the patchwork of studies looks like the patchwork of feudal jurisdictions in medieval France. Their theme has inevitably been structural: What was a typical seigneurie? What were the distinctive structural variations by region? What were the nature and duration of typical servile obligations within the regional models of the seigneurie? What was the secular impact of generalized phenomena like population pressure, war, and pestilence on servile obligations and agricultural production?

The aim of these studies is to recreate a kind of collective mentality, a *structure mentale* shaped by the material facts of everyday life. The effort is clearly an important one, although the practitioners are not always successful. The most disappointing work produced in the tradition, yet in some ways the most important, is the recent collective effort, conceived as the rewriting of Marc Bloch's contributions, namely, the *Histoire de la France rurale.* It is hard to characterize such a work as massive as the *Histoire* (four bulky volumes), but it lacks a certain anecdotal vividness and, therefore, immediacy. As Bloch's own work attests, however, the scholarly reconstruction of the characteristic structures of rural life need not lack drama or the verve that comes from occasionally mentioning real human beings.

What all the studies discussed up to now ignore is the urban environment; yet, *servitus* frequently existed in towns despite textbook assertions to the contrary. Sens was one such town in the thirteenth century. The traditional type of urban study with its emphasis on administrative matters has been of value here, but also helpful have been works on mobility in medieval French towns. Drawing partly on the knowledge that the medieval town was highly stratified, with much poverty and with many "marginal groups," historians have shown that there was still much fluidity even if the continuous vitality of urban life is questioned. David Nicholas, albeit in a broader context, and others have employed this approach. To this end, traditional data bases like records of debts are being exploited, but less for their information on economic trends than on their relevance to social relationships of dependency—of class and of caste.

The reference to class in the preceding paragraph is a fitting transition to a fifth and final variety of work that has also been of interest in this research on the Sénonais. I refer to the great and avowedly Marxist histories of lower-class exploitation and discontent. No one, whether Marxist or not, can afford to ignore the penetrating work of E. A. Kosminsky on the English peasantry which is full of insights that have heuristic value for the study of thirteenth-century French rustics or the work of Rodney Hilton, part of which treats Western Europe in general. Whether the type of exploitation and discontent explored by these scholars or the structures that underlay those expressions of dissatisfaction fit neatly into Marxist categories is a tenuous question and one we need not address. But the general point is worth emphasizing: if one does not look for social struggle it can easily be missed in a romantic evocation of the community of the vill, the world we have lost. More directly, the history of the Sénonais in the thirteenth century seems on first reading of the records from its past to have been as gentle as the landscape, without serious disturbances; but the closer one looks at incidents superficially peaceful, such as the freeing of rustics by charter, the more one discovers profound social tensions ready to explode into violence and destruction.

The studies discussed above depend on a wide variety of sources, not all of which survive or even ever existed in the Sénonais. Our guides to Sénonais records—nineteenth-century antiquaries and archivists like Maximilien Quantin—have published or inventoried a great many examples of what is available, but sometimes so carelessly that the work would have been better left undone. Still, the published materials, some of the originals of which are now lost, and the caches of unpublished manuscripts constitute a rich and diverse hoard, so rich and so diverse that the Sénonais can be an intensely revealing illustration of the process of manumission.

First in importance in reconstructing the servile regime are records that describe in concrete detail the obligations of individuals or of communities to lords. Failing such records, a surrogate is comprised of documents that describe the enforcement of these obligations and which, by doing so, refer in specific terms to the characteristics of the servile regime. Lists of income available from the enforcement of the obligations and court cases arising from disputes over their nature are also pertinent here.[29]

A second source, at least as significant, is comprised of charters of general manumission and similar charters that remove a selection of debasing obligations.[30] These legal records detail in formal language the rights granted to people formerly *de corpore* (servile) or lacking free rights of marriage and inheritance. Despite the formality of language, these manumissions, as I shall call them, give us accurate information, though sometimes only as hints, about the underlying causes of the acts. They also provide us with the names of those manumitted, and in certain mass manumissions the number of names can run into the hundreds. Where supplementary records exist, the names can be fundamentally important. Under close scrutiny the principle for the arrangement of the names usually reveals itself as geographical, a clue that they were transcribed from rent books or similar records that were routinely organized geographically.

Rich but uneven caches of charters involving conveyancing of real property also survive for the Sénonais. Charters involving only lay people are decidedly rare, but those involving religious establishments had to be recorded before the *officialis* or judge of the archdeacon or archbishop of Sens in the thirteenth century. These records survive in parochial clusters because the archives of the churches have suffered repeated depredations. Even so, they are relatively abundant; and, happily, their form is simple and more or less consistent although there is, over the course of the century, some evolution in style. Happily, too, the hands of the scribes of the *officiales* were uniformly clear and strong.[31]

Other fiscal or quasi-fiscal records are thin, again because of the depredations of the later Middle Ages and the Wars of Religion. Few formal accounts for estates or institutions survive from the thirteenth century, but those that do are enormously precious. Municipal accounts for the town of Sens, for example, surface in the 1260s. The earliest of these (from 1260) exists because the central government became interested in the extent of taxation in its good towns in the late 1250s. The *mises*, as the taxes were called, were supposed to be regulated by the crown, but at most times the crown was permissive about, not to say inattentive to, how often and in what ways municipal authorities raised money. A financial crisis during which the royal government was unable to obtain prompt payment of an "aid" that had been imposed on the towns brought about a wide-ranging investigation into municipal financial practices and, ultimately, a crackdown on municipal taxation. The first account of Sens is the fullest relic of that investigation.[32] Other financial accounts of the town and its *mises* survive from 1261 and 1262, but after that there is a lapse until 1436.[33]

To utilize this source adequately we must be fairly certain about the nature of the *mises* recorded in the account. Fortunately

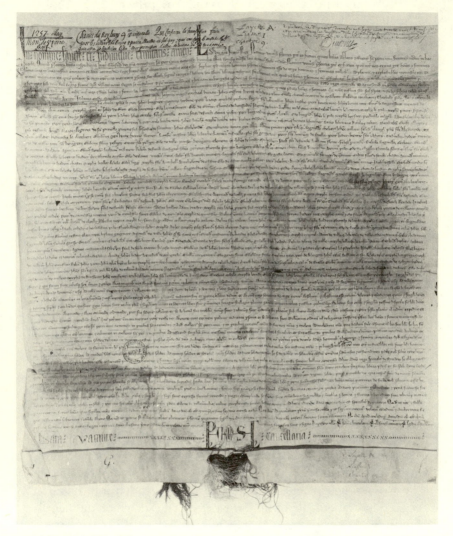

*Manumission of Serfs by the Abbey of Saint Pierre-le-Vif of Sens, 1257
(AD: Yonne, H 51 MS 7)*

the ground is firm on this point. First, the taxes were not uniform head taxes on all adults, male and female, because the assessments varied and relatively few women show up on the account (which lists several thousands of names parish by parish). The *mises* were, therefore, taxes either on movables or on hearths. The latter is almost certainly the truth, considering the standardization of sums assessed. The immunity of certain base dependents of lords from the *mises* is also certain. This immunity was not a happy fact of life to municipal authorities, but it was jealously protected by the lords.[34] The *mises* of Sens in their method of assessment and in the existence of privileged immune groups were little different from the levies imposed by other nearby communities.[35]

Traditional sources, like cartularies and chronicles, survive with some frequency from the Sénonais, but much has been lost to time. For example, the cathedral of Sens, according to an inventory of its archives in 1620, was in possession of at least eight cartularies in the seventeenth century. Of these only a copy of one has been preserved; and from the point of view of this study it is the least interesting since it is a record of the most solemn transactions, of oaths of suffragans, and of observances of abbots and abbesses dependent on the archepiscopal see. The nitty-gritty of estate management and conflicts is not prominent.[36] On the other hand, the chronicles of Saint-Pierre-le-Vif, the great Benedictine monastery, are extraordinarily full. The one dealing preeminently with the thirteenth century is an extremely detailed look at monastic politics and the monks' relations with other social groups.[37]

The most interesting, if difficult, source available is made up of the so-called obituary books and related texts. They must be treated with caution, but they profoundly reward close analysis.[38] Obituary books record the endowments of people for whom churches celebrated masses on the anniversaries of their deaths. Scribes constantly revised the books in order to maintain accurate enumerations of the tenants of the properties whose rents endowed the anniversaries. Entries, therefore, allow the scholar to identify lands (which are always briefly described) and to trace changes in their tenants. One can find out something about rents, worship at the churches, and even about the people who endowed the churches, a fact that makes the obituaries a surrogate for testaments, a type of source that has not survived in abundance in the thirteenth-century Sénonais.[39]

As individual obituaries became fuller over time, that is, as people died and their families endowed anniversaries in their name, and as new tenants replaced old, it was necessary for copyists to make new expanded manuscripts. Whenever this was done, what was retained from each existing entry was the name of the person whose anniversary was to be celebrated, the land or rents endowing the celebration, and, minimally, the current tenants. Tenants who had died or otherwise ceded tenancy were not necessarily of interest to the copyist, although many slavishly retained a record of a few former tenants perhaps in order to preserve some sense of continuity or, more particularly, where the name of a former tenant had come to be identified with the property itself.

Many other scribes simply began with tenants contemporary with them or the date of their copy. A manuscript started in, say, 1300 might therefore have lists of tenants going back to 1200 or it might have lists going back only to tenants established in 1300. This fact has little or nothing to do with the person whose anniversary was being celebrated from the rents paid by the tenants. The original endowments could easily relate to people who had died several hundred years or only one month before the beginning of the manuscript. The obligation of the historian, therefore, is to set the information on the tenants into the context of other records, especially other records of tenancy, roughly contemporary with the beginning of the composition of the manuscript of whatever obituary is being studied. Such records, of various quality and abundance in the Sénonais, require careful attention to key words in personal and geographical names. But thorough immersion in the region studied has aided in making reasonable guesses and in coming to reasonable conclusions about the meaning of the data assembled.

The obituaries, which have additional peculiarities besides those mentioned above, have played a central role in the case study that accompanies this book. Indeed, without the obituaries the book as a whole could not have been undertaken. They provide, although obviously in less tractable form, the sort of information that the Toronto School extracts from manorial court rolls and admissions to tenure and that other scholars have managed to obtain from more extensive estate *fiscalia* than survive for the Sénonais.

Other sources have been helpful in completing this research, but their special problems or benefits can be taken up more conveniently in the course of the study itself. It is to a detailed discussion of the issue of status and of manumission as a legal process that we now turn.

~~2~~

Status and Manumission in the Sénonais

All societies impose obligations on people, obligations that are frequently classified as honorable or dishonorable by those who govern society or have the opportunity to record their impressions of social life. The two adjectives are not always euphemisms for light and heavy. A medieval vassal in the twelfth century owed the onerous but honorable task of knight's service to his lord. A rustic might owe considerably less onerous labor services—three days' worth of plowing, for example, on his lord's estate—that nonetheless lowered him in the eyes of the literate minority and perhaps in his own estimation as well. Views about what was honorable and what was not could change. Before the twelfth century the profession of the knight was problematic. By the end of the twelfth century we may speak of the elevated and, often, legally protected status of knighthood.[1] It was a still later development that saw the onus of military service erode while the dignity of knighthood survived. Similarly, learned opinions on the status of rustics owing manual labor underwent considerable change. Always such labor was regarded as rather demeaning by the learned; it would have been difficult for them to think of it otherwise so long as the peasantry was dependent, in a material sense, on a seigneurial upper class. Nonetheless the opinion grew in the course of the twelfth and thirteenth centuries that obligations of manual labor and similar forms of service were not simply less honorable than some others, but that they profoundly debased one's dignity, indeed that they created a serf.

Serf is by no means an easy word. The range of meanings attached to it in the Middle Ages was wide.[2] Even in a small region like the Sénonais people could differ about what dishonorable obligations or jural disabilities were necessary and sufficient to constitute a serf. For this reason, some historians would like to push the word aside, fearing that it obscures a complex set of social phenomena.[3] We need not insist on the word here, even though it or forms of it, like *servitus* ("servitude"), were commonly used in Sénonais records. What matters is that observers regarded certain jural disabilities and obligations as signs of lower status, and they used these signs as a rule of thumb to determine, for example, whether a person had a right of access to royal courts or whether he was subject to certain sorts of taxes.[4] The people who suffered under these disabilities and obligations recognized that they were of inferior legal status; consequently, they pressed to have them removed. Manumission was the method used to respond to this pressure by the lords to whom the obligations were owed or on whom the jural disabilities depended. At least, the verb *to manumit* was used in charters relieving people of these disabilities.[5]

In the Sénonais the fundamental jural disabilities came to be considered six in number, although not everyone who suffered under any one of these necessarily suffered under all the others. The first and perhaps the most debasing was mainmortability.[6] It was hard to be both free and mainmortable, although late twelfth-century Sénonais manumissions, lacking legal precision, sometimes conjoin the words.[7] When applied to chattels, mainmortability signified that the movable property possessed by a dependent would return (or escheat) on his death to his seigneur. Such a dependent, in other word, had no heirs, in the proper sense of that term, for his chattels. Traditions of "inheritance" among rustics and in towns and villages mitigated this rigorous interpretation of mainmort. A token or not-so-token payment, such as the best beast, was the usual offering to the seigneur in lieu of full escheat when children of the deceased dependent were alive to receive the goods and were resident in the parental homestead.[8] A mainmortable dependent might by custom even alienate a portion of his chattels by will to the church—a privilege that was by no means unique to the Sénonais. Paul Hyams has discussed the same custom in England.[9] When there were no offspring and when collateral relatives wished to succeed to the deceased's goods, lords often demanded stiff fees for permission to do so.[10]

Mainmort also applied to the transfer of real property and incorporeal rights. Custom softened the law, however, in much the same way (though perhaps not quite so fully) as it did with chattels. Tenants who were personally free (that is, not subjected to mainmort *ratione personae*) sometimes occupied mainmortable tenements and vice versa, but this coupling, as we might guess, was increasingly frowned upon by the lawyers who were systematizing the rules of status and tenure in the thirteenth century. Beaumanoir, for one, insisted that inhabitation of a mainmortable tenement for one year and one day debased the status of a lay commoner.[11]

Another fundamental jural disability in the Sénonais restricted liberty of residence and freedom of movement.[12] As a corollary to this disability, the so-called *droit de suite* endowed the seigneur with coercive powers over his dependent, including peremptory rights in his holding and chattels wherever he might dwell.[13] The most talked about customary exception to the jurisdictional aspects of *droit de suite*, escape to a town and open and unchallenged residence there for the proverbial year and a day, could always be circumscribed by conventions between lords.[14] Such conventions were a leading feature of the juridical regime in the Sénonais.[15]

Whether these conventions inhibited migration is problematic. Recent comparative work has shown that even without a custom like "town air makes one free," people in a debased dependent relationship migrated to towns for economic opportunities.[16] Moreover, and more to the point, conventions in the Sénonais could be circumscribed by mutual agreement between lords and their dependents for a price.[17] The result was that the pattern of movement does not seem to have differed in the Sénonais between people suffering under theoretical restrictions on residence and others. Or, at least, a detailed analysis of the regional surnames of the residents of various parishes in Sens shows no fundamental difference between the geographical backgrounds of residents of parishes largely inhabited by people with this jural disability and those without it.[18] More work needs to be done on this complicated issue, as evidence from neighboring Champagne shows.[19]

A third jural liability in the region, sometimes regarded as the most debasing, was the array of restrictions on marriage or, to be more precise, on out-marriage (*formariage*) and mixed-marriage. The restrictions complemented and supplemented those touching residence and movement since marriage ordinarily involved some change of dwelling by at least one partner and often by both. Out-marriage was the union of the dependent of one seigneur with the dependent of another. Mixed-marriage was a union between a free person (one who did not suffer under the jural disabilities being discussed) and a person who needed the license of a seigneur to marry outside the jurisdiction of the seigneurie. The close coupling of restrictions on movement with those on marriage is explicit in a case concerning the eighteen-year-old daughter of a village mayor in the Sénonais who acknowledged before the *officialis* of Sens in 1248 that she was dependent on the cathedral chapter. This meant that she lacked the legal capacity to marry at all without the consent of her lord, to marry a foreigner (a person under a different lordship), or to reside outside the seigneurie of the chapter. As security for these promises she pledged any chattels over which she might have customary rights of disposition in her lifetime.[20]

Dependents could acquire the privilege of entering into out-marriages by making appropriate oblations to the lords concerned, but a consideration other than the amount of the oblations affected the willingness of seigneurs to grant the privilege, namely, the disposition of the seisin of the offspring of such unions.[21] Whose dependents did they become? Custom on this point did vary remarkably—even in a region as small as the Sénonais.[22] Some litigants eventually claimed that status followed the mother. Presumably, then, the law should show a preference toward the proprietary claims of the mother's seigneur over those of the father's. Others argued that status descended through the father. Under these circumstances the proprietary claims of his seigneur might be stronger. A legitimate quibble was whether the pattern of status transmission should have anything to do with such claims. Custom in the Sénonais (as in England) had a strain within it that tended to attribute the better proprietary claim over the children of out-marriages, regardless of lines of descent, to the seigneur within whose seigneurie they were born. Again, therefore, residence and restrictions on residence affected seigneurial concerns about dependents' marriages.

The way out of the problems was for the seigneurs to reach conventions among themselves, drawing on other current ideas in favor of the equal division of seisin in the disposition of the children, especially the male children, of out-marriages.[23] During the thirteenth century this type of agreement became common in the Sénonais. Ecclesiastical lords were no less exigent on the meticulous details of division than were their lay counterparts.[24] Although there was an undoubted advantage for the dependent parents in the explicitness of the contracts, the apparent lack of humanity of the documents in discussing the disposition of the single or odd male child gives substance to the pious platitude in so many manumissions that the jural disabilities we have been discussing were unnatural and vile.

Mixed-marriage presented a less tractable problem. In theory, seigneurial license and the making of customary oblations were all that were incumbent on a dependent if she (more rarely, he) wanted to marry a free person.[25] Again, however, seigneurs had a vested interest in those customs that would secure the offspring of such unions to them as dependents. Naturally, if there was demand and if seigneurs hesitated to give permission, their dependents would have been forced either to make illicit (or clandestine) unions or openly to defy seigneurial authority.[26] Marc Bloch, who contended—on very inconclusive and spotty evidence—that mixed-marriages were uncommon, attributed their low frequency to the various complications and to the sense of honor of free people that inhibited them from tainting themselves in such unions.[27] I do not know what "common" or "uncommon" means numerically in this context, but recent research has qualified Bloch's view. Observers may have regarded mixed-marriage as a calamity in personal relations, but participants, however few, were willing to endure the dishonor. Or, perhaps, it would be fairer to say that they were spurred to denounce the seigneurial regime all the more. Some scholars, as Georges Duby makes plain, now see a close relationship between popular efforts to eradicate the array of disabilities collected loosely under the generic term *serfdom* and the desire for freedom of marriage.[28]

In addition to mainmort and restrictions on residence, movement, and marriage, prohibitions on the making of an ecclesiastical vocation were typically regarded as debasing and required manumission for relief.[29] These prohibitions probably never stood alone. If a person, that is, had some other firm sign of a debased status, it followed that he could not enter orders or that he could not profess the religious life. Hence, to be manumitted in this context meant that a dependent necessarily escaped other jural disabilities besides the mere bar to a clerical vocation. No one knows whether it was difficult to convince lords to manumit so that dependents might join the church; no one knows what it cost. What is certain is that interests were complicated in this issue. The church was wary of angering lay seigneurs by accepting their dependents into its bosom without their consent; lay seigneurs, on the other hand, sometimes wanted to give oblates to the church even as clerical opinion on the propriety of accepting oblates was changing. Finally, parents who needed the labor of young children but who could ill afford to antagonize their lords might also have been of two minds about ecclesiastical careers for their offspring.[30]

In theory, seigneurs derived one of their major economic benefits from those dependents from whom they could demand labor services (*corvées*). These labor services were the unpaid or tokenly paid work required of certain rustics on their lords' demesnes for a restricted period or periods during the year. To say that such labor was an economic benefit is not to say that it was easy to obtain (even on manors) or one of the more efficient available ways to carry on agricultural production. Quite the contrary, at least partly because of tensions arising from the conflicting need of dependents to tend their own arable, lords were sometimes eager to have the *corvées* commuted to oblations of money. Secular changes in the incidence of *corvées* and commutation provide a good insight, indeed, into the fundamental trends in the development of the medieval economy. Even when and where commutation prevailed, however, the payment itself (going under various names) came to be regarded as a fundamental sign of jural disability.[31]

To discuss the pristine pecuniary obligations of dependents is to come face to face with an infamous word, *taille*.[32] Unfortunately for terminological precision, the word could be applied in other contexts than that of base dependency. For our purposes the most demeaning use of the word would be in such phrases as "taillable at will" or "taillable high and low." This form of the taille probably began as an occasional levy imposed on people already in a dependent relationship to a lord. The severity and nature of the dependency would determine, from our point of view, whether the taille, occasional monetary aid demanded by the lord for his protection of his dependents, should be considered itself a sign of fundamental jural disability. Increasingly during the thirteenth century, legists tended to regard the taille as such a sign. Consequently, both people of obviously low status and those of obviously high status who for one reason or another owed a taille were eager to be delivered from the burden. Not that the amount necessarily constituted much of a financial burden: early disputes between lords and dependents of various statuses had led to the "fixing" of tailles.[33] In the Sénonais the rate varied widely depending on prior agreements,[34] but on the whole it was reasonable.[35] In any case, in the thirteenth century the taille was no longer (if it had ever been) conceived of as a mere *tolt*, an arbitrary and deeply resented "taking," as Bloch and Guy de Valous thought. Resentment could not rest in its arbitrariness because its amount and frequency were established by custom. What resentment there was centered on the fact that subjection to the levy could be said to imply an inferior social status.[36]

Such then were the signs or liabilities that increasingly came to be articulated by some legists as grounds for denying people access to royal courts. These legists, however, misrepresented the historical reality. It would have been more accurate for them to write that the disabilities implied a plenitude of power in the lord and that his jurisdiction, therefore, flowed inevitably from them.[37] That the legists chose a juridical formula that made a person's relationship to the royal courts the issue of moment underscores the fact that the interests, power, and authority of the crown were growing apace in the late twelfth and thirteenth centuries.[38] Implicit in the statement that jural disabilities prevented some people from having direct access to royal courts is the legal fiction that they had once had such access. Failure by their lords to respect customary relationships might well have been an excuse for the crown to recover its jurisdiction, to urge the lords toward manumission.[39]

Why there should have been a movement in thirteenth-century France or in any place in any century to manumit people who were in dependent relationships characterized by the disabilities that we have been discussing is a difficult question since authority over other human beings is not a commodity ceded very lightly.

Perhaps the answer is tied up with the considerations adumbrated in the previous paragraph. Under certain precise historical conditions, lords may have been urged by economic necessity to demand the whole array of benefits that should have accrued to them in the seigneurial regime. Their dependents would have reacted negatively if these demands had violated customary norms in any way. The resolution of such disputes, disputes that presaged violence, would have necessitated the intervention of superior authorities who had a vested interest in social peace. The matter is, of course, much more complicated than this, and we shall return to it presently, but something like this scenario must have been behind the enormous number of manumissions that occurred in the thirteenth century.[40] The thirteenth-century Sénonais and its borderlands saw manumissions granted to groups of people living at Véron (1196); Vareilles (1197); Tonnerre (1211); Sacy (1214); Villeneuve-la-Guyard (1224); Montréal (1228); Vinneuf, Courson, Baissy (1228); Andrésy (1230); Saint-Florentin (1231); Noyers (1232); Fouchères (1243); Villemanoche, Chaumont, Champigny, Villeneuve-la-Guyard, Villeblevin, Dyant (1247); Perrigny (1256); Sens and its environs (1257); Villeblevin, Chaumont-sur-Yonne (1257); Chablis (1258); Monéteau, Sommeville (1263); Vermanton (1264); Saint-Aubin-Châteauneuf (1266); Saint-Julien-du-Sault (1270); Courgenay (1271); Chitry (1275); Appoigny, Bries, Bailly (1276); Vareilles (1277); Nitry, Lichères (1278); Coulanges-les-Vineuses, Baroche (1279); Isle-sous-Montréal (1279); Cravan(t) (1280); Gy-l'Evêque, Vallan, Vaux, Champs, Jussy, Migé, Charentenay, Ouanne, Courson, and a dozen other neighboring hamlets (1283); Soucy, Saint-Martin-sur-Oreuse (1283); Accolay (1290); and Evry (1290).[41]

This already impressive list is probably incomplete since records of the manumissions of individuals have not survived so well as records for groups. On the other hand, certain historians would say that the list is somewhat inflated because I have included a few so-called enfranchisements along with the manumissions. Enfranchisements usually delivered whole communities (villages, towns) from a selection of disabilities, not always debasing, and frequently either confirmed or granted rights of self-government. A manumission, it is said, delivered a person or people from the full array of debasing disabilities.[42] But the distinction, given the language of the original records, is not hard and fast. *Manumittere, dimittere, remittere, liberare, quitare* could be used in both sorts of acts.[43] The main point is this (and it explains the overlap of operative verbs in the two types of charter): an enfranchisement that includes a delivery from any one of the six jural disabilities that were characterized as debasing of personal status in the Sénonais can, for our purposes, be considered together with manumissions properly so called. Both were responses to the same urgent pressures for change in the thirteenth century.

Why did the issue of manumission become urgent in the thirteenth century? Many factors have been cited. One of the most frequently cited is the management rationalism of the lords. Medieval estate managers supposedly came to believe that the *corvée* was an inefficient form of labor, and they increasingly sought to hire their labor from the large and stable labor pool that characterized the thirteenth century, the century in which the internal medieval frontier created by deforestation and drainage closed. Moreover, since custom had eroded the benefits that had once accrued to lords from keeping people under such liabilities as those we have discussed, it follows that they would have been willing to manumit their dependents for a price.[44] These speculations may partly be true, but a slightly more transparent explanation is, I think, more powerful.

There was simply an increased need in the thirteenth century for ready capital within the seigneurial class to finance its crusading, its elaborate buildings, and its patronage of the arts. The need for new money was increasing because of the thirteenth-century crisis in fixed rents. These rents varied in name, from quit-rents (Latin *census*, French *cens*), to customs (Latin *custume*, French *coutumes*), to *redditus*.[45] By the thirteenth century quit-rents were token payments, symbolically important because they were a fundamental sign of the collectors' lordship, but, in the Sénonais, financially trivial: many were accounted in terms of pennies or parts of pennies. The word "customs" is what Sénonais scribes often wrote for payments in kind or for money that substituted for payments once made in kind. These payments, too, were fixed annual renders. *Redditus* is the word scribes in the Sénonais used to refer either generically to all sorts of rent or more narrowly to renegotiated rents. Renegotiation could take place when the biological line of customary tenants died out or when flagrant misuse (abandonment, wastage, default) permitted the entry of a new tenant; but unless the renegotiation led to an agreement to the contrary, the new rent too eventually became fixed.[46]

Ecclesiastical lords had special problems. Rents of whatever sort, when given to churches for the celebration of anniversary masses, were never renegotiable. The church that accepted the endowment was making an agreement to celebrate an anniversary (by singing mass, lighting candles, ringing bells, distributing charity to the poor) on the basis of a fixed annual return. It tried to make sure that the tenement always remained occupied so that the rent would be paid. But it had not the legal capacity arbitrarily to raise the rent or any other fixed payment connected with the endowment (although nothing could stop it from trying). The alternative would have been for churches to require endowments of land itself instead of rents, but secular governments in the thirteenth century were especially wary of permitting more land to go to the church;[47] and donors, as Barbara Harvey has shown, knew that the income from open-ended grants of land were especially liable to be misappropriated by churchmen.[48]

Fixed rents, fixed amounts as commutations of renders in kind and of labor services, fixed annual tailles—all of these contributed to the income of lords. And all were seriously eroded by inflation, a phenomenon the lords hardly understood. Thanks to the work of Gérard Sivéry we now have a pretty good index of price inflation in thirteenth-century northern France. From 1180 to 1270 the value of the French pound was eroded by 60 percent,[49] a fact that helps explain those vehement expressions of despair that we find in so many records from Sens and its environs. The abbot of Saint-Pierre-le-Vif complained in 1277 that "the rents of the treasury of our monastery are trifling and have suffered loss on many occasions."[50] An investigation of the fiscal situation of the Cistercian nuns of La Cour Notre-Dame de Michery in 1285 reported that its "rents and income (were) trifling and inadequate."[51] What Sénonais lords despaired of, their counterparts elsewhere in northwestern Europe bemoaned as well.[52]

Lords had many sources of income that were not "fixed," as Valous's work on Cluniac houses elaborately documents.[53] They strove in the thirteenth century to emphasize these sources through, for example, the careful exploitation of the banalities that gave them not only income but a preferred status in the marketplace. The ban of the mill required that a rustic's grain be ground at a seigneurial mill. The ban of wine required that the lord's grapes be pressed first and his wine sold first. The ban of the oven compelled rustics to bake their bread in the lord's oven at established prices.[54] Careful attention to exploiting the banalities was expanded into a particularly careful scrutiny of all financial rights. The cleric who prepared the Register of Revenues of Notre-Dame of Issoudun in the early fourteenth century reveals the fact nicely. On folio after folio he takes note of which rents and income varied or were negotiable yearly, that is, in his own words, which "could be increased and [alas!] diminished." He was unsure sometimes, so he repeatedly reminded himself to "look into the matter," to "find out whether there can be any more," and so forth.[55]

Especially strong or prestigious ecclesiastical institutions might successfully avoid being endowed with fixed rents. The cathedral of Sens, for example, frequently made arrangements to buy leases whose rents were open to negotiation, the anniversary to be celebrated with whatever could be made from them.[56] And some churches received special contingency grants. A charter of 1290 states explicitly that if a grant of forty shillings for a series of anniversaries could not be raised from the income of the land conveyed to a certain church, "the residual would be supplied" from a vineyard in the possession of the donor.[57]

The buying up of rents was still another mode of meeting the fiscal crunch. Such purchases meant a modest capital outlay for long-term returns, but sometimes when immediate financial demands on lords were low, they systematically chose to make these outlays as a hedge against an uncertain future.[58] In the early fourteenth century, a particular opportunity came in the aftermath of the expulsion of the Jews (1306); and it points up the intensity of the effort. For, although the crown conveyed lands and leases to the confiscated properties by auction,[59] it refused bids from ecclesiastics. Even so, they managed to circumvent the law to their advantage.[60]

The buying up of subleases was a special category of the procedure just described. If a lord leased property and after a time the tenant or one of the tenant's successors subleased a portion, the new rent on the subleased tenement was, because of inflation, likely to be larger than that for the original lease. Indeed, the older the original lease, the greater the difference would be between the two amounts. This fact could be galling to superior lords who saw people of low social status (even base dependents) collecting rents on tiny properties that were higher than the rents they were collecting on extensive properties.[61] Purchase of the subleases from sublessors for a lump sum equal to, say, thrice the yearly rent that the sublessee paid was good business if a temporarily impecunious sublessor could be induced to sell. We possess a number of instances in the Sénonais where this sort of policy of redemption (the market in chattels real) was actively pursued with modest success.[62]

Despite these compensatory efforts, the plaints of lords desperate for money or in the hands of exigent creditors driving them into shady practices are impressive and evoke a Western European

phenomenon. An abbot of Saint-Pierre-le-Vif of Sens was compelled to alienate a dependent priory in the early thirteenth century;[63] the legally questionable efforts of Cluniac houses in France,
Spain, and Italy to do the same thing have been catalogued by
Valous;[64] and it is certain that English abbots managed to carry off
similar feats.[65] But the most vivid legal example I know touches
the monastery of Saint-Pierre of Auxerre and properties it held in
the Sénonais. A series of records dating from 1258 contains the
elaborate approvals required by superior ecclesiastical authorities
for the Auxerrois abbey to effect the alienation. The house, according to the records, was being "burdened by great and urgent
debts" that were "daily increasing because of usury," and the indebtedness was propelling the monks toward "poverty." If the situation were to continue and the alienation not be licensed, "the
monastery would be destroyed in an abyss of usury."[66]

Situations such as the above, stemming from the crisis in fixed
rents and sometimes aggravated or compounded by the over-
lavish building of a church[67] or long costly litigation[68] or some
combination of these pressures, explain why so many lords turned
to manumission.[69] Several manumissions refer explicitly to the
"relief" that high-priced sales of freedom would give to the "most
urgent obligation of the debts of the church,"[70] to the "urgent necessity" of the ecclesiastical institution,[71] or to the burden of debt
on the manumitting lay lord.[72]

We should notice also the close connection between manumission as a way of raising money and as a way of affirming other
financial rights. The banalities are a case in point. They are often
carefully singled out for affirmation or confirmation in manumissions. In some instances these are the first documents in
which their precise limits are expressed.[73] Differentiated, as they
were, from the vile customs that debased personal status, the banalities were explicitly interpreted as one part of the compensation for manumission. As one Sénonais charter put it in 1196,
"moved by pious consideration" the lords "remitted . . . main-

mort in perpetuity." In return (*in recompensationem*) the freedmen "were obliged by the ban perpetually to cook at the [lords'] oven."[74]

Despite these indications, the charters on the whole do not give the need for ready money or additional income-producing rights as the principal reason for seigneurial grace. Religion is more frequently attested.[75] Historians may too readily discount these sentiments,[76] preserved in phrases like "moved by pious consideration" or in eloquent denunciations of the vileness of *servitus*,[77] described as being contrary to the law of nature and of God.[78] They may forget that in a society in which personal bonds were not mere contracts, but expressions of love, modifications in the nature of the bonds might not have been conceivable without recourse to the religious sentiment. When the count of Auxerre in 1211 delivered the inhabitants of Tonnerre in the southern Sénonais from their mainmortability, he was not speaking merely empty platitudes when he explained that he did so "cherishing a singular love" for the *bourg*.[79]

Naturally, among people as obsessed with the need to uphold customary bonds of loyalty as medieval people were, such innovation as manumission was not entirely without resistance. And even under slightly different economic conditions the trend toward manumission might be arrested.[80] In the thirteenth century itself no seigneur automatically decided on manumission or enfranchisement as the appropriate way to obtain money quickly, as the work of Jean Richard on the Burgundians indicates.[81] It was much more likely that a seigneur would prefer to retain the familiar look of his society, not obliterate ties of lordship and dependence. To be sure, indebtedness might induce him to try to manipulate or tighten up his powers over his dependents. He might seek a judgment, and fine, against them in court for failures to fulfill his ideal notion of their obligations in the past. (This, again, underscores the role of the increasingly powerful state; a lord had to show that his ideal notion tallied with legitimate custom to the satisfaction of not always friendly royal justices.) Or he might take a more aggressive stance and induce, or try to induce, his dependents to make a special payment in his behalf by a threat of court action or other reprisal. Such a procedure smacked of a *tolt*, or arbitrary taking, frequently referred to without definition in our records.[82] The only truly effective way to appreciate the complex web of emotions and motives that might culminate in manumission is a case study.

PART TWO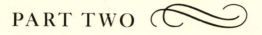

Case Study

⤨ 3

The Struggle for Freedom of the Dependents of the Abbey of Saint-Pierre-le-Vif of Sens

In the year 1240 the monks of Saint-Pierre-le-Vif of Sens elected Geoffroy de Montigny, a scion of a noble Sénonais family, as their new abbot. He was to serve the house in this capacity, as it turned out, until his death in 1282. Geoffroy's family had placed him as a youth in Saint-Pierre, the premier Benedictine abbey in Sens, with the plausible expectation that he would eventually achieve the headship, which was to be one more jewel in the lineage's crown. Already two of Geoffroy's cousins were abbots. One of them ruled the abbey of Saint-Remy of Sens, and another cousin, Guillaume Jutard, had achieved the headship of Morigny in the late 1230s and would secure that of Saint-Remy in the 1250s. Other cousins of Geoffroy, the brothers Gautier and Gilles Cornu and their nephews, Henri and Gilles Cornu, served the royal government as intimate advisers of the monarchs and as archbishops of Sens: Gautier from 1222 to 1241, the elder Gilles from 1244 to 1254, Henri from 1255 to 1258, and the younger Gilles from 1274 to 1292. The contemporary chronicler of Saint-Pierre-le-Vif, still another of Geoffroy's relatives (his nephew), relates without any embarrassment how the Cornu clergymen helped in Geoffroy's early advancement to power.[1]

The prestige of the abbey of which Geoffroy became the head was enormous. Since its foundation in the sixth century, it had accumulated rights of patronage and properties throughout the Sénonais, even as far south as Auvergne.[2] Its one real problem was its church, an *ecclesia dissipata* in the words of the chronicler. It had fallen into disrepair during the lackadaisical abbacy of one of Geoffroy's predecessors; and although there had been plans for many years to rebuild or remodel the basilica, no one had carried them through.[3] The embarrassment of the church was manifest in 1239 when the full array of the royal court visited Sens during the progression of the Crown of Thorns to Paris. The king had purchased the relic from the Latin emperor of Constantinople; and wild enthusiasm, according to an eyewitness report written by Gautier Cornu, then archbishop of Sens, greeted its reception. The king and his advisers permitted the crown to repose overnight in the abbey of Saint-Pierre-le-Vif.[4] The condition of the *ecclesia dissipata* would have been clear to everyone.

Therein lay the challenge for the young man who assumed his duties as abbot in the next year: to use whatever his predecessors had accumulated and to seek new money to bring the repair of the church to completion.[5] A few examples of the actions Geoffroy took during the long period of his abbacy will illustrate how he handled the challenge. He began by trying to find out whether everyone who owed money and services to the abbey was properly rendering them. As early as 1242 he closed a loophole that had allowed the prior of the dependent priory of Saint-Loup-du-Naud to default on his traditional oblation of hides to the abbey. Henceforth, if hides were not available the prior was to provide each of the monks of Saint-Pierre with four ells of cloth for vestments, thus protecting the general resources of the abbey from any unwonted drain.[6]

The new abbot also finally resolved a longstanding problem with the dependent priory of Mauriac in Auvergne, a matter that took up a very considerable amount of his time. The priory of Mauriac was distinguished in its own right and had been fighting since the twelfth century to assert its immunity from Saint-Pierre's pretended right to visitation.[7] But it was Geoffroy who, after long, arduous efforts, successfully concluded the matter in the 1250s, with the ecclesiastical authorities inflicting on the priory a punitive fine.[8]

The victories over Saint-Loup and over Mauriac had their sequel in victories over the dependent curate of Neuilly and the dependent priory of Sainte-Marie-d'Andrésy. In the first case ecclesiastical authorities condemned the curate in 1265 to pay an annual rent of forty shillings to the abbey, a rent which, though instituted as early as 1217, had not been rendered for many years. Abbot Geoffroy succeeded in assembling the records in order to bring the matter to a decisive judgment.[9] In the second case the abbot argued successfully that the monks of Sainte-Marie should continue to contribute to the maintenance of the windows of Saint-Pierre's church even if the windows were replaced in the rebuilding program: this seems the most reasonable interpretation of an order to Sainte-Marie in 1277 to donate twenty pounds *parisis* yearly for the upkeep of the new windows.[10]

The maintenance of the repaired church of Saint-Pierre became uppermost in the abbot's mind as he grew older; one of the ways he sought to provide for it was to get control over income-producing property. Necessarily this put him in conflict with other ecclesiastics who were seeking noble largesse for their own purposes. A revealing episode involved the abbot's purchase of the woods of Noeriaus from a prominent noble, Lord Dreu of Traînel. In December of 1262, however, Ansel of Traînel, the constable of Champagne and Dreu's uncle, retook possession of the woods by *retrait lignager*, the custom that gave near relatives first right to sales of family property. What makes it certain that this was a struggle for noble patronage is that Ansel did not care about keeping the woods, but he insisted nonetheless that they not pass to Saint-Pierre-le-Vif and promptly granted them to the abbey of Valuisant, one of the institutional rivals of Saint-Pierre in the Sénonais.[11]

This setback for Abbot Geoffroy was more or less isolated. In his relations with the municipal authorities of the self-governing commune of Sens, for example, he was very successful at exploiting opportunities for getting money. The opportunities arose because of the longstanding hostility of the commune and the monastery, which originated in the opposition of an earlier abbot, Hébert by name, to the very establishment of the commune in the twelfth century. Hébert's murder had resulted in a huge fine that the communards were still paying off in the mid-thirteenth century—or so it seems.[12] No love had been lost between the commune and the abbey since Hébert's time. Particularly galling to the municipality was the privileged jurisdiction that the abbey enjoyed in the outlying parishes of the city. Called the Bourg-Saint-Pierre, this jurisdictional enclave suffered recurrent threatening gestures. There are records of violent incidents from the stormy period when the idea of a municipal commune first made its appearance (1156, 1186, 1189) and even after the royal government had confirmed the enclave and its absolute immunity from communal penetration (1213, 1225).[13] Abbot Geoffroy did not endure these affronts to his dignity patiently. He sued in the royal courts over a long series of infractions; and in 1259 he won a group of judgments in the Parlement of Paris, the highest royal court, condemning the commune to pay the abbey damages for its violation of the jurisdiction of the bourg.[14]

It was Abbot Geoffroy's lay tenants and base dependents, however, who were the really crucial element in his effort to get the enormous sums for rebuilding the church. Thus, his relations with them were nastier and more complex than any sketched so far. The problems began when the abbot or his assistants discovered that certain families who had once suffered the full panoply of jural disabilities in the Sénonais, that is, who had been *homines de corpore* of the abbey, had descendants who were not fulfilling their obligations. Indeed, some of these descendants were not simply failing to fulfill their obligations, they were denying their bondage: "We [the abbot and monastery of Saint-Pierre-le-Vif] were saying that the aforesaid men and women were *de corpore* . . . which the said men and women were not confessing." It was this that became, according to the contemporary formula, "a matter of contention," that is, the foundation of a social struggle.[15]

We may dismiss the notion that this claim was mere convention or a threat never associated with any particular family or families, as sometimes occurred in other situations.[16] The records available to us explicitly name two families that made the claim: that of Hugues Le Roux d'Arces and that of Pierre Ribaut. Both families resided not in Sens but in the privileged town of Villeneuve-le-Roi,[17] the present Villeneuve-sur-Yonne, one of the very few successful foundations of the twelfth century. Part of Villeneuve's success was due to the fact that people who lived there enjoyed an array of immunities and royal protection denied many nonroyal new towns in the region (such as Villeneuve-la-Guyard and Villeneuve-l'Archevêque). Moreover, its location was superb; it is hard to imagine why a major town had not grown up on its site before. The consequence of these facts was that Villeneuve-sur-Yonne attracted a great many immigrants to whom usually the full benefits of residence in the town were routinely granted. To live there, one might suppose, was a presumption of liberty,[18] but probably an unfair presumption.

Consider the case of Hugues Le Roux d'Arces. While going through the records of the abbey, one of the monks undoubtedly came upon a "recognition" dated August 1220. It referred to a period on the eve of Hugues's taking up residence in Villeneuve-sur-Yonne. Hugues, his wife Adeline, and their children lawfully acknowledged that they were *homines de corpore* of Saint-Pierre-le-Vif and were, therefore, liable to a taille of two shillings annually, according to the customs of the Bourg-Saint-Pierre where they were then dwelling.[19] Having sworn the recognition, Hugues was permitted to remove with his family to Villeneuve-sur-Yonne, where he prospered. At his death his survivors were able to provide endowments for the celebration of his and his father's requiem masses on 3 January. The money for the celebrations came from an annual rent assigned to the monastery of twelve shillings from property of which Hugues had been the lessor near the leprosarium of Auxonne: ten shillings went directly to Saint-Pierre's monks, twelve pence to charity, and another twelve pence to the bell ringers of the abbey church.[20] Again, according to contemporary attestations, the descendants of Hugues—inheritors of his wealth—were acting as if they were free in the 1250s. Among them were Hugues's son Simon Le Roux and Hugues's grandson Jean, the son of Etienne Le Roux.[21]

The case of the Ribaut family is similar. A recognition of 1221 included the information that Pierre Ribaut and his (first) wife had been negotiating to reside outside the domains of the monastery of Saint-Pierre-le-Vif. On pain of a huge fine of two hundred pounds *parisis*, forfeiture of their chattels, and forfeiture of the chattels of certain of their guarantors, the couple publicly acknowledged themselves *homines de corpore* of the monastery and subject to its taille, whereupon they removed to Villeneuve-sur-Yonne.[22] The wife who swore the recognition with Pierre predeceased him, and he later married Agnès of Evry, the dependent of a different seigneur. Agnès outlived her husband.[23]

The size of the fine potentially leviable on Pierre attests to the immensity of his wealth. We also know that he held property scattered through several villages and over a wide area of the Sénonais.[24] Moreover, his family endowed his anniversary mass at Saint-Pierre on 2 November with annual rents of eleven shillings from two pieces of property at Bachy near Serbonnes of which Pierre had been the lessor.[25] He was buried in some honor, in the abbey churchyard near the door of the treasurer's cell.[26]

At least one recent historian, J.-L. Dauphin, has stressed the importance of these two family histories in comprehending Saint-Pierre's concern for its bondmen. He has argued, working from suggestions originally put forward by Maurice Prou in the nineteenth century, that what Abbot Geoffroy did in order to express

the concern of his monastery, namely, manumit its dependents—
all the dependents, according to Dauphin—was a "radical remedy" to the lingering and vexing problem of people taking up residence illegally in the royal town of Villeneuve-sur-Yonne where,
after a brief open habitation, free status was automatically conferred.[27] The "radical remedy" had a positive side; it brought the
abbey six thousand pounds *parisis*, a sum greater than any institution had ever before made from manumitting a group of people.[28]
But despite the elevated sum, the manumission was really the
conclusion on the part of the abbot and his monastery that they
were failures in curbing illegal migration to Villeneuve-sur-Yonne.

I believe that this argument is wrong. First, neither the Ribaut
nor the Le Roux d'Arces had moved to Villeneuve-sur-Yonne illegally. They had been granted permission to do so by the abbey,
and they had publicly affirmed the continuity of their status despite their removal to the town. To be sure, illegal migration to
Villeneuve-sur-Yonne was a problem for Saint-Pierre-le-Vif[29] and
for other seigneurs as well.[30] But the problem presented by these
two families was of a different sort. It is clear that the monks had
put too much confidence in the recognitions that they had exacted
from the families. A period of lax leadership, the same sort of
leadership that had permitted the abbey church to fall into disrepair, and bad recordkeeping had compromised the abbey's position. A kind of de facto freedom must have been lived by the
families. By 1257 they were asserting it de jure.

Dauphin also contends that all the dependents of Saint-Pierre-
le-Vif achieved manumission in 1257, further proof, it must be
supposed, of the radical nature of the remedy. But this too, I
think, is wrong. He has evidently misunderstood the manumission which, as we shall see, most certainly does exclude some
dependents of the abbey, including numerous families concentrated on its manors where it continued to collect tailles: Paroy,
Volgre, Champlay.[31] But if Dauphin is wrong, what is the truth?
How did the abbey of Saint-Pierre-le-Vif come to the idea of
manumission and by what principle or principles did it limit its

application? I have hinted at the answers to these questions, but much more needs to be said.

It was bad enough for Abbot Geoffroy to learn that a few families far from the center of his power, at Villeneuve-sur-Yonne, were not fulfilling their obligations. It must have been more of a shock to discover that people living in Sens were doing the same. Records show that beginning in at least 1239 a man named Jean Letardi paid taxes to the commune of Sens as if he were a citizen of the town, but Saint-Pierre-le-Vif ultimately claimed him as one of its *homines de corpore*. At least, it did not manumit him until 1257.[32] The fiscal records of the commune also reveal that the municipality demanded taxes from Jean's neighbor Humbert Foace as a citizen of the commune from the 1240s. He too was not to be manumitted until 1257.[33] As late as 1249, Saint-Pierre-le-Vif itself was making contracts with certain free people whose status it would soon challenge after the careful search of its records: Jean Mouflet; Thécie, the widow of Félis Charpentier; and Thécie's son Pierre.[34]

Who were these people? A few details are certain. Humbert Foace and his family took their name from the vineyard known as Foaca on the Rue Nouvelle in a wealthy part of Sens in the neighborhood of the residence known as The Knight's House.[35] Humbert possessed a stone house himself which his children inherited.[36] Assessments on him for communal taxes were very high, a good indicator of his standing.[37] The only other of the Foace family known to me is Jacques, who seems to have been reasonably well-off. After his death the monks of Saint-Pierre-le-Vif celebrated his anniversary on the ides of July from the proceeds of an annual rent of three shillings *parisis* that he had formerly collected as lessor of a vineyard. From its description ("behind the house of the late Eudes, the cleric"), it has been possible to determine that the vineyard was in a stretch of choice enclosures along the *rû* or irrigation ditch known as the Mondereau.[38]

Jean Mouflet, another of those challenged in their status, makes an especially interesting case. In 1249, before Abbot Geoffroy apparently realized the need to challenge Jean's status, he made an agreement with him that qualifies Jean unequivocally as a "citizen of Sens." By the agreement Jean and his relatives by marriage recognized the assignment to Saint-Pierre of the annual rents of a vineyard leasing for six shillings *parisis* per year. Jean's late father-in-law had assigned the rents of the vineyard to Saint-Pierre in his last will and testament. Abbot Geoffroy also agreed in the recognition to re-lease the vineyard directly to Jean and his relatives.[39] In the recognition of 1249 Jean, who would now possess a vineyard, is described as a leatherworker (*cordubenarius*) or, better, leather merchant, for other evidence reveals that he had a major shop in the *cordubenaria* neighborhood of Sens which he leased from the cathedral chapter for the exceedingly high rent of fifty shillings per year.[40]

Jean Mouflet's associates in the recognition and lease of the vineyard in 1249 were his wife, Douce; his mother-in-law, Thécie; and his brothers-in-law Gui and Pierre (a minor). The father-in-law whose property the recognition referred to was Félis Charpentier, a man who had been of immense standing in Sens. The first clear evidence of him dates from 1236, at which time he was already prominent enough to act as a guarantor for Yvon de Aula and his wife of a lease to them of two orchards (*ortos*) in the parish of Saint-Préer of Sens. The landlord was the cathedral chapter.[41] Félis appears to have been not only a business associate but a neighbor of Yvon's family (the "de Aula") in the quarter of Sens known as the *Pargamenaria*.[42] Félis also provided for the celebration of his anniversary at Saint-Pierre. The *Book of Revenues* of the abbey (a book probably made to try to improve the recordkeeping at Saint-Pierre) describes the property endowing the anniversary, 2 October, in precisely the same terms as it was described in the recognition of 1249, to which at one point there is even a reference. The rents, however, are lower in the recognition (only five shillings *tournois* as compared to six shillings *parisis*), which explains why Saint-Pierre had briefly taken the vineyard into its own hands for direct exploitation (*thesaurarius tenet*). In this period the monastery was looking for new tenants who would pay the higher customary rent. It found those tenants in Jean Mouflet and his Charpentier in-laws.[43]

The evidence thus far assembled clearly places these families in the category of the Ribaut and the Le Roux d'Arces of Villeneuve-le-Roi, that is, among the economically substantial segment of the local population. I presume, as others have argued, that they would emerge as the leaders in any struggle with their putative monastic lord. Certainly, the name of Jean Mouflet lived on long after the struggle was over. Nearly a half-century later people recalled him and presumably his leadership in opposition to Saint-Pierre-le-Vif.[44]

These examples do not mean that every person who claimed to be free of Saint-Pierre's lordship but who could have been challenged in that claim in the late 1250s was necessarily well-off. There is, for example, the case of Pierre Bourgignon. He had a relative named Eudes Bourgignon, a "free" man who was also "manumitted" in 1257, living only a house or two away from him in one of the parishes in the Bourg-Saint-Pierre. That Pierre and Eudes were treated as free men before 1257 appears from the fact that they were assessed as such by the commune in 1252. Their occupation was leatherworking, but unlike Jean Mouflet, they were poor. Pierre was unable to pay his communal taxes in 1258 or 1259; ultimately part of his business passed to Eudes.[45]

Nonetheless, cases like Pierre's aside, a significant number of people do seem to have had the resources and the determination to defend their claim to be free. The really puzzling question remains, How had they managed to live freely within the shadow of the abbey's power? Consistently I have alluded to the lax leadership of the abbey before Abbot Geoffroy's election in 1240, but perhaps the leadership was more than lax. Perhaps these *homines et femine de corpore* had purchased their exemption from the taille or had received some other privilege that they equated with an elevation of status, but that lawyers might have been more reluctant to assert. Or perhaps mixed-marriages had taken place and the uncertainty, or the conflicting views, of how status descended in the Sénonais led to assertions of liberty that the predecessors of Abbot Geoffroy had not gainsaid. But however it occurred, the situation facing Abbot Geoffroy was complex. I doubt that he wanted to commit himself to the expensive and time-consuming effort of establishing the dependency of these people, even if he threatened to do so. Part of the evidence that would have been used against his case was his own transactions with them as free people. Similarly, his opponents could have had only bits and pieces of documentary proof, most of it prescriptive rather than declaratory. For them to go to law would mean to risk degradation of their (de facto) status and a future of large personal fines for having fraudulently avoided their obligations in the past.

Out of this morass arose the spirit of compromise. Something might be worked out whereby the abbey would recognize its pu-tative dependents' liberty (would manumit them) in return for an appropriate sum of money. Here was an opportunity, indeed, for Abbot Geoffroy to obtain a really large sum with which to effect the repair of the abbey church. But the decision to compromise was only the first step. The discussions would have to take place under neutral arbitrators. But who was neutral? Ecclesiastics seem to have been either related to Geoffroy or hostile to him because of his efforts to get money from them or to secure the noble largesse that would otherwise go to them. Municipal authorities were hardly to have been approached either. Indeed they must have been pretty much open about their support of the abbot's oppo-nents, who claimed after all to be *cives Senonenses*. The mayor of Sens at the time of the dispute was Etienne Dallemant, a member of a wealthy family (perhaps the wealthiest in the city)[46] on the verge of joining the country squirearchy.[47] In the thirteenth cen-tury they served in a number of high government posts.[48] They also seem to have dominated as landlords in the city.[49] Their over-all standing caused people to seek them out to arbitrate disputes.[50] But the mid-1250s when Etienne Dallemant was mayor was the time when Saint-Pierre-le-Vif and the municipality were in court against each other about violations of the jurisdiction of the Bourg-Saint-Pierre.[51] Moreover, other members of the Dallemant family were intimately connected with some of the people opposing Saint-Pierre on the issue of their status: Jean Dallemant and the widow of Thiérry Dallemant had done tenurial business with the Le Roux d'Arces and with another of Saint-Pierre's putative dependents, Etienne Bousart; and a member of the Ermite family (also a dependent family, according to the abbey) attested the purchase of a fief by Guillaume Dallemant in 1270.[52]

It might have been possible to find some other important bourgeois or ecclesiastic to arbitrate, but the parties to the dispute found an acceptable choice outside these groups. They settled on Etienne Tâtesaveur d'Orléans, the royal *bailli* of Sens.[53] The prestige of a high royal official had much to commend it, and since *baillis* could not be native to the areas they administered, they stood above the tangle of local interests.[54] But there was a more compelling reason to turn to the *bailli*. The path to him was probably suggested by the king or by someone in his entourage. The circumstances were these. The king often visited Sens. He had been married there in 1234; his wife had been crowned in the cathedral. He had visited again in 1239 on the occasion of the arrival of the Crown of Thorns in the city and its repose at Saint-Pierre-le-Vif. He visited still again in 1248 on his trip south to lead his crusade.[55] More important, soon after his return from crusade in 1254, the king visited the Sénonais again and appointed Etienne Tâtesaveur as *bailli*, an appointment followed up, in 1255 and 1257, with a systematic investigation of administration in the Sénonais, including matters pertinent to the royal town of Villeneuve-sur-Yonne.[56] In this context it should not strike us as surprising that the king despatched a special deputy, the knight Gilles de Villemarchez, to help Etienne Tâtesaveur arbitrate the dispute between Saint-Pierre-le-Vif and its putative dependents,[57] some of whom lived at his Villeneuve.

The negotiations were not easy, probably because Abbot Geoffroy was trying to obtain enough money through the manu-

mission virtually to rebuild the basilica of Saint-Pierre.[58] Whatever he may first have demanded was probably considered too
high by his opponents. But this sticky point was resolved in a
very clever way. There were many people living in Sens who were
incontestably *homines et femine de corpore* of the abbey and who
were obviously apprehensive about the more exacting lordship
that distinguished Abbot Geoffroy's leadership. Moreover, all
through the rural areas of the Sénonais the abbey had dependents—one family here, another there—the result of scattered
donations and commendations across the centuries. Much evidence suggests that lords usually found it difficult to control and
exploit people of this sort. The abbey also had concentrations of
bondmen on its estates, at places already mentioned such as
Paroy, Volgre, and Champlay, as well as at Bray-sur-Seine.[59] One
could argue whether the obligations, particularly the labor services, of these groups of people should be retained. Abbot Geoffroy decided (or agreed) to manumit the scattered dependents, but
he would retain control of the others.[60]

It was a matter of some importance to describe with precision
the sweep of territory inhabited by these scattered rural dependents and consequently covered by the manumission. The region
formed a triangle about fifty kilometers on a side. It was bounded
by the Seine and the Yonne and by an imaginary line running
from Villeneuve-le-Roi, on the Yonne, to Nogent-sur-Seine.[61] As
clear as this description is, however, most writers if they mention
this manumission at all attribute to it a very minor importance because, they say, only one or two villages were affected (Saligny
and Mâlay-Saint-Pierre) and what to them could only have been a
handful of people in Sens. In fact, about two hundred fifty people
were affected in the city. This misimpression ultimately derives
from the chronicler of Saint-Pierre's notice of the manumission in
the so-called *Book of Relics*, a handlist of the holy objects in the
abbey's possession. The chronicler, Abbot Geoffroy's nephew, describes the area of his uncle's concern as the Bourg-Saint-Pierre of
Sens, Saligny, and Mâlay, and adds the phrase, "and all the way

up to the Seine."[62] The regional meaning of this phrase only becomes clear on reading the longer and rather more tedious manumission.

Everywhere in the Sénonais the terrain is suitable for both cereal husbandry and grazing. Wheat, barley, and oats are specifically noted in the sources and pastures too are well represented.[63] Within the villages and towns and especially in the hillier parts of the region, viticulture prevailed. Sens was no exception, at least in its outlying parishes.[64] In the Middle Ages there was no necessary community of interest, however, between grain growers and viticulturalists. Saint-Pierre-le-Vif by offering to free its dependents in Sens and Villeneuve-sur-Yonne as well as those scattered in homesteads throughout the northern Sénonais threw people of very different economic backgrounds together. What is germain to any reconstruction of the negotiations is the fact that grain growers and viticulturalists were not enjoying equal prosperity in 1257. As the chronicler of Saint-Pierre tells us, the year 1256–57 in the Sénonais was a very bad year, a time of "hunger and high prices."[65]

The reference to hunger, that is, to insufficiencies of grain, is extremely significant. Imperfect but disturbing English figures show wheat prices in 1257 as 233 percent of those in 1255 (the base year); and they were still climbing, though much less steeply, through 1258 when they averaged 265 percent of the 1255 base figure.[66] We are compelled to draw on English figures because French yearly data are woefully incomplete. Even so, some very sketchy evidence assembled by Gérard Sivéry from northern France suggests a dramatic rise in grain prices by 1259 in Normandy, by 1256 in the Laonnois, and by 1260 in Champagne.[67] Together with the English material these data point to the most pronounced and geographically extensive constriction of the grain market in northern Europe (as measured merely by price inflation) in the thirteenth century. The situation reacted substantially upon other vital productive sectors of the economy and, as the Baronial Revolt in England suggests, upon politics as well.[68]

The hunger and high prices had considerable impact on the emotional history of Sens, for mechanisms to deal with want were not very well developed in the city. An alms house existed, but the surviving records of its operation are thin.[69] In any case, not much of the regular income of ecclesiastical institutions was earmarked for charity. Of the endowments for masses, for example, at the Cathedral of Sens in the thirteenth century, less than one hundred shillings from the total of three thousand was assigned to bread for the poor (*in pane pauperibus*).[70] A curious record from 1257, an arbitration of burial rights between two ecclesiastical institutions, provides us with a hint about what life was like in Sens in that year. An excess of deaths of children (boys up to age 14 and girls up to age 12) at the little (*minor*) hospital of Sens had led to a dispute about the appropriation of burial fees.[71] It may be that these deaths were related to the lower resistance that must have accompanied undernourishment.

The impact of the economic crisis, as bad as it may have been, was uneven and temporary. The laboring urban poor and grain farmers must have suffered more and longer than viticulturalists for several reasons. First, the viticulturalists were tied in to an international market. Some of the wines produced by the small family vineyards in the Sénonais were consumed locally, as records of regional trade establish,[72] but the Sénonais, the natural geographic northward extension of the Auxerrois wine-producing region, also exported far and wide. To be sure, the five-hundred-year dominance of the Auxerrois in the so-called battle of the wines ceased in the thirteenth century when the whole region east of Paris, from Laon in the north to the hilly villages south of Auxerre, began to lose its importance in the European economy. Nonetheless, people continued to respect and purchase the product of this region long after Bordeaux emerged as the dominant center of viniculture in France. During the period of interest to us, however, barges in numbers still plied the length of the Seine and the Yonne with the wines of Auxerre and Sens.[73] Following these rivers, the huge casks with "that cash crop *par excellence*," as

Rodney Hilton has called it,[74] made their way northwest to Paris, Rouen, and from the depot at Rouen, to England. Overland, caravaners transported the vintage to Champagne. And by the river Oise there was penetration northward through the depot of Compiègne to Picardy, Artois, Flanders, and Hainault.[75] This access to a national and international market surely dampened the negative effects of lower per capita local consumption during the economic crisis of 1256–57.

Moreover, the sort of weather that had probably cut grain production and raised prices may not necessarily have been harmful to grape production,[76] although what really matters is precisely what sort of weather ruined the cereal crops. And general speculation about northern French weather patterns in the thirteenth century, no matter how interesting or important for other issues, really does not speak to this question.[77] Still, the direct and immediate injury was suffered by those who tended the grain and those laboring poor who purchased bread with the greater part of their earnings.

In terms of the arbitration that was going on over the contention between the abbey of Saint-Pierre-le-Vif and its dependents, the effect of the crisis was muted. To be sure, the abbey, despite the diversity of its income from tithes, fines, tailles, oblations, rents, tolls, and the sale of agricultural surplus,[78] could not have been insulated from the economic conditions of 1256–57. This may have been a determining factor in its abbot's decision to seek a compromise with his antagonists. But the leaders of his opposition were reasonably well-off in any event, and, more important, the extension of the proposed manumission to hundreds of acknowledged *homines et femine de corpore*, many of whom were viticulturalists, was possible precisely because this group was weathering the grain crisis tolerably well. Certainly they, too, like the urban poor, were paying higher prices for or eating less bread, but this did not undermine their willingness or ability to join in the purchase of manumission. And in the end, as the chronicler assures us, Abbot Geoffroy de Montigny got paid.[79]

If the agreement of the viticulturalists still makes sense despite the economic difficulties of the mid-1250s, problems persist in understanding the feelings of those whose primary income came from the sale of grain. Yet, two cases are illustrative of what took place in these critical years: that of Jean Malebeste and that of Thibaut Munier. The organization of the list of people ultimately manumitted places the homesteads of Jean and Thibaut near each other. The list also suggests that Jean shared his dwelling with two kinsmen, probably his sons or brothers, Eudes and Félis Malebeste, who achieved their liberty by the same instrument as he.[80] From other records it is possible to identify the location of these homesteads in more detail. Thibaut Munier held of the abbey of Saint-Pierre a plot of land that rented for ten shillings *tournois* situated near the *Botoarii*, the abbey's tanning mill. It was undoubtedly given over to grain production; no vines are mentioned. He worked this property with his son Jean Munier. He eventually gave up part of it (three-tenths, if the allocation of rents is a key) to a different cultivator, leaving him and his son with a pecuniary obligation to the abbey of seven shillings per year.[81]

The names of Thibaut Munier and Jean Malebeste occur together in a rather different source from the manumission. A scribe of Saint-Pierre-le-Vif employed a parchment to make a few preliminary sums that he could then transfer to the general fiscal account that he was preparing. This sheet, one of many similar that have survived, has been entitled by a modern archivist, "Men of Paroy, Volgre and Champlay," because three of the four lists on the parchment denominate the dependents of Saint-Pierre liable to the taille at these three places which, from 1257, were retained as taillable villages despite the manumission. The remaining list is different; its contemporary thirteenth-century heading evidently baffled the archivist. Yet, on the whole it is straightforward. It reads: "The ones who owed money from charity."[82] Thibaut Munier's name is on this list and his debt (that is, the amount of money he owed or got as charity), as we might expect, was equivalent to the annual rent of his property, seven shillings. To put it another way, the abbey temporarily pardoned the rent that was due on Thibaut's holding. On the same list Jean Malebeste figures for a temporary pardon of six shillings for his holding. Conditions in the area of Thibaut's and Jean's lands and of the lands of the other seven rustics on the list were so bad as to make payment of their rents impossible during (the likely year) 1257 or the year or two thereafter.

From the point of view of the monastery the pardons made good sense, for they kept tenants, whether free or unfree, on their holdings at a time when it would have been difficult to induce responsible farmers to take up vacant plots. But the matter is more telling: the respite allowed Thibaut and Jean a temporary peace of mind without which they could not have joined in the purchase of manumission. We have here, then, just one incident among many that must have complicated the negotiations, for assuredly the monastery insisted that Thibaut and Jean include themselves in the final accord. I assume the men promised to contribute to the cost as soon as they recovered their financial solvency, although the only evidence in favor of this assumption is the enrollment of their names on the manumission itself.

Once it had been determined precisely who was covered by the manumission, it became necessary to define the substantive limits of manumission. Abbot Geoffroy naturally retained those powers over his tenants that did not imply the "yoke of servitude," as the manumission brutally described their former dependency. To the chronicler of Saint-Pierre the essence of the yoke was mainmortability; when that jural disability was removed the dependents became free.[83] The act of manumission was more detailed: the dependents became free in status when they became "free and immune of forage [and] stallage [dues or labor involving fodder and stalls], residual personal jurisdiction, *corvées*, *tolts*, and tailles"; when they could "dispose of their property as free men, selling it, giving it away, alienating it at pleasure . . . , excepting terrains that were leased from (the monastery)"; when "they could marry people outside the seigneurie and they and their children could assume clerical orders." Their freedom also revived when they began to enjoy liberty of residence.[84] Scholars have inflated the significance of free residence because of the explicit role of people who lived at Villeneuve-sur-Yonne in bringing about the manumission. It is only one of many enumerated in the manumission, however, and was not the one that a contemporary observer, like the chronicler, would have thought was essential. Late ancien-regime lawyers, committed to a careful delineation of the crown's rights, also gave more emphasis to the problems of Villeneuve, that is, to problems that had been associated with the king's demesne property.[85]

Although manumission implied or explicitly granted certain liberties, it confirmed other obligations. Those who remained tenants of Saint-Pierre were still obliged to bake their bread at the ovens of the abbey and grind their grain at its mills, although because of a quirk of local custom, a few had to bake but not grind.[86] Again, ancien-regime lawyers in Saint-Pierre's pay tended to magnify these aspects of the limitations of the manumission in later struggles over the extent of seigneurial banalities. Those struggles were occasioned by the fact that Saint-Pierre had mills at two different places with very similar names (Maillot and Mâlay) which are spelled almost exactly the same in medieval Latin. In 1703 the lawyers, whether deliberately or not, tried to read the thirteenth-century manumission as a charter of banal rights at Maillot (which was inaccurate).[87]

Some disabilities were obviously removed by manumission; others, like the banalities, were confirmed. Yet there was a gray area in between where reasonable human beings could differ. The manumission hints at the interchange between the two parties. Once it tells us that a few people would have to continue to render services to the abbey that were specifically territorial, not personal. Only if they moved would they be immune from such services.[88] But, evidently the abbey also asked that its former dependents aid it in making a yearly oblation to the archbishop of Sens. This seems to have struck the arbiters as a nonterritorial obligation like a taille and, therefore, demeaning. The manumission in final form suppressed the aid.[89]

The manumission conceded what I earlier called "residual personal jurisdiction." This is rather a free translation of the phrase *placitis generalibus*. This must refer, however, to jurisdiction *ratione personae* because elsewhere in the manumission, the drafters very specifically affirmed the territorial jurisdiction of the abbey: "Likewise the aforesaid manumitted men and women and their heirs as long as they dwell and reside in our lands, vills or franchises and in our Bourg-Saint-Pierre-le-Vif will be justiciable just as our free men."[90] Undoubtedly the building and room where the free men of Saint-Pierre were justiciable were the same as those once used for the *homines de corpore*, but we know just enough about procedures in Saint-Pierre's courts to establish that treatment of causes differed according to the status of the litigants. For example, with regard to the admissibility of testimony, Saint-Pierre had been conservative, not permitting the testimony of bondmen in free causes.[91] Having become free, the *emancipati* no longer suffered this indignity.

One last technical point: the intervention of the crown forces us to recall that the newly freed men and women of Saint-Pierre enjoyed a status defined not only by the manumission but also by the already existing law of the Sénonais, law enforced under the eye of the crown's officials. There could be quibbling over this or that provision of the manumission, but such quibbling would be resolved by the king's courts, to which the *emancipati* now would have redress.[92] In a word, there were limits to the quibbling because the crown recognized, and when appropriate used its power to enforce, a widely agreed upon set of liberties for free people that were enumerated in a whole range of documents besides manumissions.[93] There still remained some problematic aspects to "manumission," but there was really no way for the abbey lord to reestablish its personal lordship by any sort of arbitrary action.

The residual complications of manumission will occupy us in part 3 of this study; some of those complications will have immediate relevance to the fate of the freedmen of Saint-Pierre-le-Vif. But a word or two should be devoted to summing up what has been learned in this investigation, and what some of the implications are. In the first place, six thousand pounds *parisis* was a great deal to pay. We must remind ourselves of the peculiar circumstances in which the struggle took place. The men and women who were eventually manumitted were at odds with an abbot pressed for money and determined to get it. As I tried to show, we can obtain some sense of the character of Abbot Geoffroy, but I do not know whether he felt constrained always to stay within the law. Even if Geoffroy's only aim was to exact as much as legitimately possible from the dependents of his monastery, that aim was still obviously hostile to men and women who thought they were free or who had been acting as if they were and to many others who had become accustomed to an easygoing lordship. Moreover, there was an edge to Geoffroy's actions in those days. He felt cheated of what was rightly his and his monastery's by these people. He had himself been seduced by their comportment into doing business with a number of them as if they were free.[94]

In these circumstances the 366 people who were enrolled in the convention of 1257 could have had no doubts about their future under the abbot of Saint-Pierre. They could have had no doubts that he would, given the opportunity, demand damages for transgressions of their status in the past. He had not hesitated to confront ecclesiastics and bourgeois officials who opposed him. Few of the bondmen could have been tempted simply to run away—to abandon home, family, and friends for the life of a wanderer—though that is the textbook image of the oppressed medieval bondman.[95] These were real people trying to survive in the familiar world they knew. Here, if anywhere, there arose that "feeling of insecurity" that could envelop those in servitude and that Marc Bloch correctly termed "very cruel."[96] On reflection, we might hastily suppose, perhaps Abbot Geoffroy settled too low. Who can say how much his opponents might have been willing to pay to evade his lordship?

We might look at the situation from the other side, however, and ask, How close did his opponents, beset by their unhappy economic situation, come to rising up against their enemy or of threatening his establishment? This too was a theme of medieval social relations in the Sénonais, as shown by the murder of Abbot Hébert of Saint-Pierre-le-Vif when he opposed the formation of the commune of Sens in the twelfth century. Moreover, the thirteenth-century chronicler of Saint-Pierre recalls and laments numerous illegal acts, such as thefts, against the abbey.[97] If we expand our vision ever so slightly, we find contemporary records of violent depredations in the monastic properties of one of Saint-Pierre's rivals, Valuisant, and thefts of precious objects at the monastery and on the properties of another competitor, Sainte-Colombe of Sens.[98] But we have been saved the task of describing how the social struggle of the men and women of Saint-Pierre-le-Vif in 1257 became even a local demonstration as happened in so many other places,[99] because the forces of royal arbitration intervened and succeeded in preserving the order of life in the Sénonais.[100] The underside of urban life particularly, which has been so vividly described by Esther Cohen and Bronislaw Geremik for Paris,[101] and which threatened to reveal itself in our sources as well, was thus banished again from the historical record and perhaps even mitigated in historical reality.

PART THREE

Complexities of Manumission

4
Arranging to Pay

Behind any manumission there is likely to have been a significant tale of discord. Manumission did not put an end to all the tensions. Indeed, by thrusting people into a new set of relationships, it created new sources out of which tensions might grow. Community standing, tenurial relationships, pre-existing bonds of marriage, and situations of dependency other than those considered debasing were all transformed by the change in juridical status brought about by manumission. The process of paying for manumission and a cluster of uncertainties about the precise interpretation of what was paid for are wonderful indicators of the socioeconomic complexities incidental to the simple juridical act of achieving "freedom." The issue of arranging to pay, which we shall take up first, cannot be divorced from other financial and nonfinancial matters. We need to recall, for example, the many pressures on lords who granted manumissions and the complicating use of words like *manumittere* and *liberare* in the charters. Factors like these might lead us to be cautious about whether arrangements to pay ought to be broken down into a set of subcategories according to the technical nature of the grant. We must remember, too, that much is lost after seven hundred years. The picture, at best, will be fragmentary, sometimes puzzling, always lacking the certainty that is the goal of all research.

The Sénonais, being a region largely devoted to the cultivation of grapes and the marketing of wine, had an advantage for many of its inhabitants faced with the necessity of raising large sums of money. That advantage lay in the possibility of securing loans on grape futures.[1] This rather sophisticated procedure necessitated the active role of a major financier. Kathryn Ryerson has identified the same procedure being employed by middle men in grain in southern France.[2] Richard Kaeuper has studied it with respect to wool production in England.[3]

Access to a major financier was the least of the problems of Sénonais residents. Sens itself was a center of both productive or long-term and consumer or short-term credit. The first necessity in most instances was long-term credit.[4] Lords who demanded lump sums for manumission did not encourage delays, whether they asked for 60 l. t., 1,500 l. t., 3,200 l. t., or 6,000 l. p. (7,500 l. t.).[5] To be fair, as we shall see, they sometimes allowed installments (large installments).[6] To be more than fair, there may have been some gentleness in the occasional provision of a grant that certain pieces of real property as payment for manumission need not come into the manumitting lord's hands until after the death of the freedman.[7] On the whole, however, they wanted quick payment, which only a financier could provide.

A financier's or middleman's arrangements with the freedmen covered by a manumission probably permitted a somewhat lengthy schedule of repayments, with interest, partly because arrangements were made with so many individuals at once. Sometimes the length of time permitted for repayment must have been considerable because total individual contributions to the lump sums were so high. How high? Let us assume that the purchase prices listed in manumissions precisely matched the real outlays of the freedmen, though this is an underestimate since we are leaving aside interest charges. Where lords manumitted (enfranchised) whole villages, the grants rarely give the numbers of individuals affected.[8] But other grants do. The list of 366 people manumitted by Saint-Pierre-le-Vif seems to break down into about 50 to 60 family groups with many lone individuals on it as well. The average payment owed by each family every year for the twelve years over which the purchase price of six thousand pounds *parisis* was to be paid in five-hundred-pounds-*parisis* increments would then come to about four pounds or so *tournois*, though the calculations to establish this fact are complex.[9]

A contribution of four pounds per year would have had little effect on some families that were manumitted in the thirteenth century; but for many it would have been unpleasant, and for all of those on the margin of economic well-being it would have been nearly disastrous. The universe of wages in the Sénonais saw a well-paid forester employed by the cathedral chapter of Sens make as much as six pounds a year,[10] not including perquisites like firewood, which had substantial monetary value.[11] The median wage of various royal guards in the thirteenth-century Sénonais was higher than this, but still little more than one or two shillings per day, or, given the likely number of workdays, about twenty-five pounds per year.[12] A family's contribution to its manumission, therefore, was probably sufficiently large to be a strain on the typical budget.

To be sure, a family budget is not merely contingent on a breadwinner's wages or the marketing of his crop, more especially not in a rural or semirural setting. Wives and daughters sold surplus produce, and young resident sons could have worked at odd jobs, part-time or full-time, in the orchards, willow thickets, alder groves, and small forests in the Sénonais,[13] as beaters, charcoal burners, woodcutters, tanners, potters, pickers, and so forth.[14] The whole matter of typical medieval household budgets is complex.[15] Nonetheless, since rents for choice properties in the Sénonais were about forty shillings a year,[16] a family contribution of four pounds (eighty shillings) to the purchase of manumission must have had an inhibiting effect on financial risk taking, even for otherwise economically comfortable tenants. This is an issue worth pursuing. We shall take it up again in the context of consumer credit and the land market.

The lords who manumitted, however, could not have been much concerned with the impact of their demands for large sums of money on individual families. They wanted to be paid. And if they were not paid on time—precisely on time—they inflicted penalties. When the lay and ecclesiastical lords of Chablis delivered the inhabitants of the town from mainmort in 1258 for 3,200 pounds *tournois*, they insisted that missing any one term of payment (these varied in length and, thus, in amount from 100 to 500 pounds) automatically incurred a 100-pound interest penalty.[17] The abbot of Saint-Pierre-le-Vif precisely enumerated the penalties incurred for lateness in paying any part of the purchase price of manumission: 1 pound per day.[18] Other lords, like the abbey of Sainte-Colombe of Sens, played the role of rigorous enforcer with equal vigor, in matters of wide financial import.[19]

The enormous financial burdens on the seigneurs in the thirteenth century meant that many lay lords and ecclesiastical institutions simply could not wait for their money. Certainly few were capable of underwriting loans by which their former dependents could purchase manumission. An exception occurred in perhaps the most famous (and, I think, eccentric) example of manumission undertaken in France in the thirteenth century, namely, that by the cathedral chapter of Notre-Dame de Paris with its dependents at Orly. The chapter seems to have played an unusually active role here, which gave it leverage over expected harvests and vintages and tenements.[20]

Exceptions aside, those who granted manumissions could not ordinarily take an active role in underwriting the loans that paid for them. Who could? The richer bourgeois of Sens could certainly provide loans. Members of the Dallemant family often stood surety for the financial obligations of other bourgeois. The role of Gaudins Dallemant in this respect needs to be emphasized since, if the mere extent of his sureties is an indicator, he was thoroughly to be depended upon in such matters. He stood surety at least ten times for other bourgeois. A kinsman, Bertrand Dallemant, stood behind another. And about twenty other cases are easily documented with priests and perhaps a guild backing the debts of delinquents.[21] Because of the position of Sens as a center for trade in fish, salt, wine, cloth, pelts, fruit, cheese, thread, horses, leather, almonds, and salted meat, we can be certain that the forms of raising and providing large loans were well known.[22] The communal charter gave traditional freedom to merchants and mercantile activity,[23] and there were three fairs—called Saint-Leu, Saint-Thibaut, and Popelin—that catered to this activity.[24] The city itself did not disdain to find a creditor from whom to borrow a large sum to pay its debts,[25] and if there was need to go outside of the Sénonais, the fairs of Champagne in the thirteenth century and Paris itself were eager for business and were not distant. At the fairs the contact would have been Guillaume Dallemant, *civis Senonensis*, who served many years as guard of the fairs.[26]

Records of specific requirements of payment for manumissions substantiate still further the fact that middlemen played an active role in providing the large sums required. In 1257 the abbot of Saint-Pierre-le-Vif, for example, required payments of 500 pounds *parisis* a year for twelve years either directly to the monastery in Sens or into its account with the Hospitallers at Paris, the latter a procedure that would have required the mediating role of a Parisian financier.[27] Since little has survived on the banking operations of the Hospitallers (unlike the Templars), whether the freedmen used this alternative remains unknown.[28] Another example: the inhabitants of Chablis agreed to have thirty-nine of their number act as "sureties, and principal debtors, and payers" of the purchase price (3,200 l. t.) of their delivery from mainmort, payable (at the fairs of Champagne) at Provins. This arrangement demonstrates that existing local forms of surety and pledging were readily adaptable to the extraordinarily large sums occasioned by such conventions.[29] The freeing of residents of Saint-Julien-du-Sault in or slightly before 1270 seems to have involved similar procedures.[30]

In concentrating on large lump sum payments and the arrangements to secure them, our focus has been on the lords, but wherever financiers or sureties played a role, they must have made parallel sets of arrangements with those manumitted.[31] Similarly, when the lords themselves decided to seek some other form of compensation than a large lump sum payment, they had to make arrangements directly with their former dependents. These arrangements give us valuable information about the ordinary engagements of ordinary people to pay for freedom and the effect of those engagements on their lives.

Several lords, for example, made their grants conditional to an agreement to pay a high though fixed annual tax usually but not always per household. Precise amounts and tariffs varied depending sometimes on the power of a lord in exacting banalities or perhaps on the perceived financial health of a community or the strength of the resistance of a community. One frequently encounters the sum of twelve pence (one shilling) in areas where the taille, which was being lost, had evidently been low,[32] a characteristic more common in the southern fringes of the Sénonais and the Auxerrois where the region shaded off into Burgundy.[33] But amounts as high as ten shillings plus four bushels of grain per household per year may be discovered.[34] Even the twelve pence figure can be misleading. The one just cited had a late penalty payment attached to it that was five times higher than the tax.[35] In the manumission of several hundred people of Soucy in 1283, the imposition of an annual hearth tax of twelve pence was supplemented by the freedmen's cession of rights in 202 arpents of woodland adjacent to existing properties of the lord. The Sénonais arpent was roughly equivalent to one acre.[36]

Often the new tax was tied more rationally to the wealth of the new taxpayer. In 1214 Ascelin, the lord of Merry, used the manumission to establish certain of his rights in the vintage of his freedmen and to assure a substantial increase in future rents in any new arable.[37] The count of Champagne, when he delivered his people in several Sénonais villages from the taille (and mainmort) in 1228 and 1231, imposed, in one instance, an annual tax of four pence a pound of the value of each tenement and in a second, an annual tax of two pence a pound on each tenement plus an additional six pence a pound on the value of movables. Precise arrangements were made so that these valuations could be determined by dependable local authorities selected by the lord from among the inhabitants, although individuals who had the cash or could borrow it could buy themselves out of the annual tax for a lump sum.[38] In 1279 Burgundian lords who had dependents in the Sénonais made similar arrangements: a variable tax was imposed from two to fifteen shillings per homestead depending on its value, with valuations made by four individuals chosen by the lords and the community.[39]

Such sliding scales varied remarkably. In 1271 the permitted scale of assessments ran from twelve pence to two shillings according to the grant for Courgenay; the lay lord of that village, however, required a penalty payment of five shillings for lateness, payable at his pleasure.[40] In 1279 the lord and representatives of the people of Coulanges and Baroche created a sliding scale up to twenty shillings; locals carried out the valuations, locals whom the lord carefully screened.[41] In 1283 the bishop of Auxerre employed a variant of these procedures in a grant to some of his Sénonais rustics. All he wanted was one hundred pounds a year from the 166 people whom he delivered from the whole range of jural disabilities that described base dependency. Six of these people guaranteed the payment in the traditional form of surety. On their own they then made the individual assessments.[42]

In the wide selection of grants discussed, the amounts required must have differed considerably from one household to the next. Inevitably many people sought small loans to cover their expenses either for the new annual taxes or for the apportionments resulting from long-term loans from sureties and financiers. The grants may have relieved the financial obligations incident to debasing jural disabilities, but it is not to be supposed that this relief entirely offset the new obligations, at least in the short run. We must recall two facts: (1) these people retained many nondebasing obligations; (2) as free people they incurred well-established obligations from which their former disabilities had insulated them.

The data point irresistibly to the conclusion that the transformation in status was financially precarious if not bleak for people with modest or low incomes. To illustrate, a dramatic increase appears in the number of tax delinquents on the communal rolls of Sens from 1252 through 1259, that is, in that complex period when the city and the region were beset by the grain crisis and when there was a spate of regional manumissions and enfranchisements.[43] By 1258, the rolls show that there were over 1,000 defaulters on the municipal tax, whereas the number had never risen much above 500 before. Indeed, in the most recent *mise* before 1258, that of 1255, the number of defaulters was only 358 throughout the city. Of the 1,090 defaulters of 1258, a certain number was made up of people manumitted only the year before. The *mise* of 1259 lists 1,823 defaulters with a commensurate rise in the number of freedmen. Let us now descend from these aggregate figures to concrete details.

In the tax of 1258 we find among the delinquents the freedmen Pierre Malebeste of the parish of Mâlay-le-Vicomte, who owed five shillings, and Jean Coiffète of the parish of Saint-Savinian, who was unable to pay the minimum assessment of twelve pence.[44] We find in the same predicament in 1258 coparishioners of Jean and also freedmen, Thibaut Fillon,[45] Gilles Longue Dame,[46] and the stepson of the widow of a man named in our records (manumission and tax list) simply Maurice. That the Maurice is the same person in both lists is clear from the situation of the name in both geographical lists relative to that of another freedman, Jean Letardi.[47]

Meanwhile, plagued by the demands of the crown for more and more money—especially to pay an indemnity occasioned by

Table 4.1   Defaulters on Municipal *Mises* of Sens

Year	Defaulters
1252	509
1254	524
1255	358
1258	1,090
1259	1,823

the Treaty of Paris of 1259[48]—the communal government of Sens levied still another tax in that year that produced another crop of defaulters.[49] Every freedman who appeared for the first time as a defaulter in 1258, with the exception of Pierre Malebeste, failed to pay in 1259. Jean Coiffète, Thibaut Fillon, Gilles Longue Dame, and the stepson of Maurice's widow were in default for the very minimum.[50] Moreover, some freedmen who had been able to meet their tax obligation in the first year of their freedom were unable to do so in the next. The record of the levy of 1259 adds to the growing list of the impoverished Félis Cartaux of the parish of Saint-Savinian as a defaulter on the minimum assessment.[51] Also incapable of meeting the obligation was Maurice's widow, who now joined her stepson in default.[52] Still another freedman identified as a defaulter on the minimum tax assessment was Raoulet Le Lavandier.[53]

At the time many of these people were manumitted, their spouses were dependents of other lords. To protect rights of inheritance, a tricky business as we shall see in the next chapter, these spouses had to have their manumission purchased. But this was possible only where lords were amenable. In such instances, they too became susceptible to the array of financial exigencies described earlier, at least for formerly mainmortable tenements over which they had customary rights of dower. Since control over this property rested with the husbands during marriage, it was the husbands who, as a formal matter, became responsible for any of their wives' taxes that the latter were obliged to pay as a result of losing their immunity. In the specific case of the communal taxes of Sens, we may point to the freedman Etienne Trumiau who was responsible and fell into default for the minimum assessment on his wife's property in 1258 and 1259.[54] Jean Letardi was a defaulter for his wife's assessment of five shillings in 1258, but he managed to reduce the outstanding arrears by half in 1259.[55] Jean Trumiau could not meet the assessment of three shillings on his wife's holdings in 1258, but he too managed to reduce this by half in 1259.[56]

The arrangements made by Jean Letardi and Jean Trumiau to reduce outstanding arrears by half were not at all uncommon in these years. I count at least seventeen other instances in their parishes alone. It seems reasonable to conclude that the financial situation in the Sénonais was rather broadly perceived as being precarious by 1260. In other words, local society could not sustain rigorous demands from all parties (creditors, tax assessors) for payments of outstanding debts. The sense of financial strain persisted for many years. By 1262 the commune of Sens was virtually bankrupt as outstanding arrears reached 1,153 pounds.[57] The "bad debts" of the abbey of Saint-Jean-lez-Sens, to use another test, became particularly troublesome in the years 1265–72, or so the arrangement of the accounts of its cellarer seems to suggest.[58]

The answer to the financial pressures for the ordinary borrower was recourse to small-time lenders, whom our documents call usurers. No account books of such lenders have survived. But to a degree this lacuna can be offset by other evidence. The best comes directly from the thirteenth-century chronicler who first called our attention to the mid-century as a time of "hunger and high prices." This remarkable observer also recalls the plague of usury. He tells us that the archbishop of Sens from 1254 until his death in 1258, Henri Cornu, can be credited with a most vigorous campaign against usury in these difficult mid-century years. He was a "lover and sustainer of the poor," who "issued sentences of excommunication against individuals manfully throughout the diocese and city."[59] Our chronicler goes further: "some say that he died by poison." Or, as later medieval enthusiasts put it: a conspiracy of usurers suborned one of the cleric's servants to poison him.[60]

The precise and manifold details of the network of small-time or short-term credit that helped sustain people in the period of financial readjustment that accompanied changes in personal status remain shadowy, like the proof of murder alleged against its organizers. Clerics like Henri Cornu might fulminate against Christian usurers; kings like Louis IX might move decisively against Jewish communities that provided distress loans.[61] Nevertheless, not many particulars can be put to this theme. The records of archepiscopal denunciations, let alone punitive action, are thin.[62] And, although the Jews of Sens could easily have financed the manumission in 1200, the economic health of their community was steadily eroded in the course of the thirteenth century.[63] I assume that by the mid-century Jews were taking precautions to make sure that records of their lending activities could not be found, especially after the 1240s when the king's wrath became evident. Investigations into these matters in other parts of northern France reveal that the Jews were very circumspect about their credit activities in the latter part of the century. It is a real misfortune that similar Sénonais investigations have disappeared, although they may await discovery even yet.[64]

Although the arrangements to pay for manumission were often complex, we should not be led to conclude that the actual making of payments was inevitably at risk. The fact is quite the opposite. So far as I can tell, not one of these manumissions was tainted by any substantial failures to pay. Whether the middlemen were reimbursed as successfully as the lords is less certain. Only local court records could inform us, and they are sketchy at best. But the important point is: the lords got paid and their dependents got free. We are left to wonder, however, whether some lords desired to make money from manumission and failed to convince their dependents that the sum demanded was worth it and, also, whether dependents of some lords were frustrated by seigneurial traditionalism from even taking the first steps toward freedom.

Before we make any final judgments about manumission, we must consider certain other questions that affected the financial aspects and may help account for shifts in the incidence of manumission in general. Poor drafting of charters, for example, could put the financial position of freedmen in jeopardy. Desires to enter the land market, to give another example, needed to be set off against other pressing concerns, largely financial. Let us begin our discussion with an illustration of poor drafting.

The story opens with the successful effort of a large group of men and women of the village of Sacy to achieve deliverance from mainmortability in 1214.[65] Other inhabitants in the village who were under the *manus* of a different lord were not thus privileged until 1236.[66] Indeed, they may have been inhibited from concluding their own negotiations because of the problems that confronted the freedmen of 1214. This earlier group appears to have been involved in a dispute with their seigneur, the lord of Merry, about what part of their vintage they owed to his overseer, or perhaps whether they owed any at all. The overseer clearly had responsibility to supervise the vines of the seigneur and to protect the ban of his wine. By the convention the parties agreed that a rather stiff contribution of one-fifteenth of the vintage of the freedmen would go the overseer.[67] This compromise somewhat offset the relief that delivery from customs like mainmort was to provide. In the still expanding economy of the early thirteenth century, however, the way to overcome this dilemma was by expanding holdings and planting more vines—in this case, on woodlands that the seigneur made available. Realizing the time it would take to turn new "assarts" into productive vineyards, he allowed a respite of rents for six years until 1220, when in compensation he was to impose a high fixed rent on the new plots.[68]

Such respites of rents for new holdings were not uncommon; there are instances in which other Sénonais lords permitted them as well.[69]

Difficulties attended this arrangement because local lords, including the lord of Merry, were patrons of the monastery of Reigny and had endowed it with woodland properties or rights in woodlands in and around Sacy.[70] The lord of Merry's permission for assarting which he had given to the rustics of Sacy turned out to violate certain of his previous grants to Reigny.[71] The monks eventually initiated a law suit seeking damages.[72] In the dispute that ensued both parties strove hard and at great expense, rustics against monks.[73] The monks, however, had not insisted on their rights, it is easy to determine, until the rustics were successfully turning the woodlands into productive arable. This seems certain because in 1220 the bishop of Auxerre, the ecclesiastical superior of Reigny, intervened decisively against the monks. The document that records his intervention is called a compromise. In fact it is a virtual surrender. Reigny gave up its law suit; it accepted the fact that the existing arable should remain in the hands of the rustics of Sacy; and it accepted that the residents could convert to arable anything that they had already purchased. The only restraint put on the rustics was on further purchases.[74] Is it too much to suppose that the determined opposition of the inhabitants of Sacy, already burdened with the levy on their vintage and the expenses of a difficult court case, suggested such a resolute intervention by the bishop? Naturally, it would not have been the attitude of the rustics alone that produced the intervention, but it must have been an extremely significant factor. There is a hint, too, that the lord of Merry put pressure on the monks to capitulate.[75] Whatever the details, for the freedmen of Sacy, the period of financial adjustment after the delivery from mainmort was made even more problematic and expensive by the poor drafting of the document.

The case of Reigny and the rustics of Sacy is not unique. With the ease and efficiency of modern recordkeeping, we are wont to be suspicious of such lapses of memory where financial rights are at issue. And yet what seems to have been true is that, as with modern title insurance, clerks had to make provision for the possibility of unknown or unsuspected claims. Mistakes happened with all types of property and at all levels. In May 1246 the king, for example, granted the right of dead wood in a royal forest near Orléans to the nunnery of Voisins, but in November 1259 he was compelled to amend the grant because his clerks had not recalled it before he sold part of the forest and all rights in it to another lord.[76] In 1257 a case in the Parlement of Paris recorded the plight of a husband, wife, and nephew who had purchased their manumission from a knight in order that they might enter a leprosarium. In point of fact, as it turned out, these people depended on the king. Thus, their manumission was null and void. Graciously, however, he permitted them to stay in the house if they so wished.[77] Repeated problems like these in the Sénonais[78] may explain why the seigneurs of Chaumont confirmed a manumission of 1247 in 1257. They considered a decade to be sufficient time for all residual difficulties to have arisen.[79]

Besides the defective manumission and its implications for the financial situation of freedmen, another major concern was the balancing of their interests in freedom against the on-going necessity or desire to control or expand their tenements and plots. The evidence is plain that the financial situation of freedmen in the first years following manumission was sufficiently precarious to inhibit efforts at consolidation and expansion of property holdings. Indeed, it appears that the very purchase of manumission stimulated the alienation of holdings for ready cash, holdings that, after the crisis years, the freedmen jealously desired and with great effort redeemed. I have traced a few revealing examples of this complex of issues as they touched the people in and around Sens who achieved manumission in 1257.

In general, there was a dearth of activity among these people in the landmarket in the first five years after manumission. It is hard to footnote nothingness, but the fact of the nothingness is

suggestive. Not until 1262 do we find evidence of renewed interesting activity in the landmarket from members of this group. In
that year five married couples from various neighborhoods of
Sens who had been united in their recent struggle for freedom
(four of the husbands were freedmen) took out a lease on five arpents of vineyard on a vacant holding. The landlord could rent
the holding at its "market" value since it was abandoned; and he
managed to exact the extraordinarily high rate of forty shillings
per arpent. The lease authorized contingency liens on the vineyard being let and on the movable and immovable property that
the couples already had. The inventory of that property shows
them to have been reasonably well-off.[80] Adam Piat and his wife,
Isabelle, possessed three-quarters of an arpent of vineyard in the
field of the late Drago contiguous to the vineyards of Isembard de
Vanne and of Adeline, the widow of Pagan de Cappis. Jean Piat
and his wife, also named Isabelle, held one-half arpent of vineyard at *Corveia* contiguous to the vineyard of Jean Lenfume and
that of Ménard de Bourg-Saint-Jean. Jacques Ermite and his wife,
Belissende, worked an unspecified amount of land near the new
bridge of Sens between the land of Guérin de Fago and that of
Pierre de Viel-Château. Pierre de Moustier and his wife, Isabelle,
possessed a house at Rudesse between the house of the late Eudes
Mâlay and the Almonry. Finally, Etienne de Moustier and his
wife, Héloise, authorized a lien on their plot at Pymard Elm between the property of Etienne Bellemère and that of Jean Gros.
The repetition of surnames plus the clustering of these names on
the manumission of 1257 suggest that this acquisition was probably a consolidation, perhaps even a reconsolidation, of family
holdings, after the immediate financial pressures of the transition
to freedom had begun to wane.

Another nice example is that of Eudes Reborrier and six other
individuals who entered an agreement not unlike that just described. They did so in 1269, twelve years after manumission, the
date coinciding with the final payment of the twelve annual installments that the lord had required for the act of grace. No

longer having to bear the burden of his contribution to the purchase of manumission, Eudes joined with his friends to lease nine
arpents of undeveloped land on which they intended, as the lease
states, to plant vineyards or build houses as they saw fit. Eudes
had two of the eight shares in the property, that is, twice as much
as any of the other parties. The rent was fifteen shillings per arpent since the land was undeveloped. If we were correct in our
earlier calculations that the head of a family probably paid about
four pounds (eighty shillings) per year in this manumission, then
Eudes's commitment of thirty-seven shillings in this lease was
more than offset by the evaporation of the debt incurred by purchase of his freedom. Following the guidelines of the canon law,
the default clauses of the lease permitted defaults to run for two
years in succession before foreclosure because the land was undeveloped. Everyone knew that the investment to make it profit-
able would be considerable, and no one wanted to see it fail for a
trivial reason.[81]

There is evidence that the properties leased in the two agreements just described were retained by the contracting parties or
their heirs and were worked profitably years later. As usual it is
not easy to prove this, but by concentrating on individual lessees
in the obituary book referring to these properties (Adam Piat in
the first; Pierre Geîte, an associate of Eudes Reborrier, in the second) we can trace the holdings over many many tenancies, including the children and a second wife of Adam and a daughter, with
the charming name of Babelée, of Pierre.[82]

Success in acquiring and working land was by no means assured merely by waiting or by cutting risks through associations
with others. This is nicely demonstrated by the case of Gilles
Boons, probably dating from about the same time as that of
Eudes. Gilles became one of a pair of lessees who paid a rent of
five shillings *parisis* for a vineyard of unspecified proportions.
Gilles' part was the larger, three-quarters of the whole (three shillings nine pence). Because the rent was low in comparison to
those already cited, I am inclined to believe that this was a prob-

lematic vineyard to begin with and that effective exploitation probably required some large capital outlay, possibly to repair some damage. Gilles and his associate could not make a go of it: when they vacated it, the lessor, interestingly, could not readily find new tenants, a resonably good indication that something was not quite right with the plot.[83]

Another freedman, Laurence de Ruelle, did not associate with anyone, but he too seems to have waited about twelve years (that is, until after his last contribution to the purchase price of his manumission) before he began the series of negotiations which led to a consolidation of his family's property. This complicated set of transactions, in fact, was not confirmed until 1273. It took place in two stages. First, Laurence took up a vacant quarter-arpent of land on the outskirts of the suburb of Sens known as Mâlay for a rent of six shillings. It was obviously a choice property given the high rent.[84] Then his wife, with her own property, and his son Pierre, a freedman like himself, as the putative heir of his mother's holding, also made an exchange at Mâlay with a major possessor there, the Cistercian nunnery of Notre-Dame-du-Lys, which was located near Melun.[85] Was this consolidation successful? If the future position of Pierre is a test, it must be said that the arrangements improved the financial position of the family. Pierre went on to be a respected member of the community. He was sufficiently wealthy in 1285 to provide cartage to the royal army with a value in excess of five pounds *tournois*, a very considerable sum; and when he died a few years later (but before 1298) his family arranged the celebration of his obit for an endowment of ten shillings *tournois* a year.[86]

To this list can be added the case of the Gaignart family. No precise date can be given to the transaction encountered here, but as we shall see the ground of belief is firm for holding that it accords with the other cases. Claire Gaignart was the wife of Hylaire Gaignart. She was manumitted in 1257; her husband was not included in the manumission since he was dependent on a different lord.[87] It is on the occasion, some years later, of Claire's death that we find evidence that her family had the resources to engage in a major set of property transactions free of the residual financial burdens of manumission. They endowed an annual mass in her memory for two shillings *tournois* drawn from rents paid by sublessees of theirs of a small vineyard at Chaliel, northeast of Sens. According to the rents, the exploiters of the vineyard had divided the holding into four equal shares when the plot left the direct exploitation of the Gaignart clan. By the time of the endowment of Claire's mass, it is clear that the family had already managed to regain control of one of these shares: it was in the hands of Jean Gaignart. But a widow named Anne held the three remaining shares. We cannot be privy to the negotiations, but something like the following must have occurred. When the family of Claire Gaignart endowed her anniversary with the sublease, they must have asked the new lessor to put pressure on Anne or in some way urge her to vacate her tenancy. Perhaps because she was bereft of the labor of a husband, she consented; and other relatives of the Gaignart family, with the nursery rhyme names Jacques and Gilles, were admitted to tenancy. For a time at least they had secure tenancy, with a relative, like Thibaut Gaignart, routinely succeeding to the holding or part of it.[88] In other words, the Gaignart family had once lost a portion of their patrimony by subleasing it, possibly at the time when the financial burdens occasioned by manumission were most intense and seemed to require this alienation. Later, having recovered their financial solvency they managed to reconsolidate their holdings in the old familial pattern.

Most frequently historians reconstruct the transforming process of manumission by purchase as if it were a one-act play, whose protagonist was economic—even proto-capitalist—rationality in estate management. I have tried to avoid this, for the reality was quite different. To be sure, rationality did have its part to play if by rationality we mean the lords' concerns for profitability, not efficient productivity. Nonetheless, social struggle, custom, and fiscality were the fundamental contributors to the action of the drama, sometimes inhibiting seigneurs, dependents, or both from successfully concluding manumissions, sometimes spurring them on. When David Nicholas writes accurately that a few seigneurs had to force their rustics to purchase freedom,[89] we should not be misled into conjuring up a hidebound group of peasants afraid of all change, even as centuries later they are all supposed to have been frightened of potatoes and hot-air balloons. The Sénonais evidence is eloquent that serious people in a real world, desperately wanting freedom, knew that their indebtedness would be heavy if they got it, knew that the likelihood of unspecified residual rights complicating their lives was too great to be ignored, knew, finally, that the financial price of freedom might mean putting even their patrimonies at risk. The wonder, perhaps, is not that a few balked, but that so many played out their parts in a drama whose epilogue might last longer and be of nearly as much consequence as the play itself.[90]

⟨ϸ⟩ 5
Residual Problems

Legal issues intruded into the lives of recently freed people not merely as adjuncts to questions of financial solvency. Whenever freedmen carried out an activity or exercised a power that a manumission had not explicitly permitted them, the law might be invoked against them. To preserve balance here, it would perhaps be more proper to say that some interpreters of manumissions might believe and, if necessary, argue in court that these grants did not permit certain activities or concede certain powers; for there were always at least two sides to the question. Each party naturally appealed to "the law" to uphold his own point of view. Each thought or said that he thought that the law was on his side. But however sure or unsure the parties or their lawyers were about what the law meant, the law to which they appealed was in fact an interpretable text or the interpretable record of a set of customary, though often seemingly contradictory, behaviors that required judges and suitors for case-by-case application. In other words, the law, despite its wonderful formality of language, was fluid and changing.

It is a bit pale and misleading to characterize the process described above as the evolution of the law, a phrase that suggests an almost detached and certainly positivist development. Instead, the appearance of fluidity, change, and reaction arises from the fact that in large measure the legal history of manumission was contingent on social realities. Did a manumission permit this or that disability to be imposed? Did it confer this or that capacity? Answers to these questions did not depend, except marginally, on internal legal logic, but on the willingness of freedmen to resist the disability or fight for the power and on the success of lords to enlist the force of the crown to defend their interpretation of manumission. The conclusions in these struggles were never foreknown; and we distort the dynamic uncertainties of human relationships in the past if we treat them schematically or as incidental to the evolutionary logic of the law. Sénonais evidence is revealing on two topics of relevance here: clerical vocation and the effect of marriage on status descent.

I believe that early thirteenth-century people were not as clear on the meaning of manumissions made to people who wished to enter the church as historians have made them out to be. It was understood that a man could be "manumitted" to enter the priesthood or that a man or woman could be manumitted to enter religion as a monk or nun, but it was not established for certain even in the mid-thirteenth century Sénonais whether such a manumission was absolute or conditional or whether, having once entered religion, a person could ever be degraded again to base jural dependency. Legal historians frequently write as if (and lords usually argued that) the point of conditionality and degradation was well-established. Those manumitted into the bosom of the church, however, did not routinely think their manumissions were conditional, even if it should happen that they abandon the church. Such a conclusion, at least, seems to emerge from a consideration of their behavior.

Let us begin with a somewhat problematic instance recorded in documents prepared in 1254. In December of that year Geoffroy d'Evry, the son of the late Hayer d'Evry, acknowledged, as I read the recognition,[1] that his father had been "manumitted in order to receive the tonsure and the clerical order." His father, it appears, had been freed many years before, probably by a charter which did not explicitly put a condition on the manumission. Hayer evidently did not find the church congenial; he left it, married, and had a family. His lord insisted that the manumission had been "on condition that if he should give up the clerical tonsure, he would revert to his pristine condition as a man of the [cathedral] chapter," his former personal lord. It had taken the chapter years to get Geoffroy, Hayer's son, to accept its interpretation of the manumission, powerful evidence that the original charter did not include any explicit attestation of the chapter's interpretation. This recognition by Geoffroy remains problematic because we do not know under what pressure he yielded a point that his father had refused successfully to acknowledge until his death. Nonetheless, in 1254 Geoffroy agreed that he would "serve the said condition" of dependency without complaint in the future. The lord who secured this agreement filed it where it made the most sense, that is, with other records that, as we shall see, were being assembled to establish precedents about status descent. They well knew that they were trying to establish a custom or strengthen one, not merely enforce an agreed-upon but broken custom.[2]

A second instance comes from records that date from 1268. In that year Jean, the son of Guérin dit Roijon of Soucy, promised that if he married or gave up the clerical tonsure, he would revert to his prior dependent status. So far this looks like proof of an already established custom. But this is misleading: Jean had already been manumitted; and he had not regarded his manumission as conditional. He had apparently got a hearing in secular courts over the efforts of his former lord, an ecclesiastic, to reexercise its lordship over him, a fact that suggests Jean had made public his intention to marry. His hearing before secular authorities evidently failed; he agreed in 1268 to abide by a prohibition enjoining him from citing, vexing, or in any way molesting his lord on pain of the loss of all his goods. His acknowledgment of this sanction is proof that he could not sustain his argument that a manumission into religion carried with it a fundamental conferral of "free" status that could not be undone by prior conditions to the contrary.[3] But it is equally important to notice that he had not hesitated to argue this position. Apparently the legal situation in 1268 was not much more certain than it had been in 1254, although the failure of the secular courts to uphold Jean's view profoundly undermined what little future it might otherwise have had.

What gives Jean's case even more interest is that it arose in Soucy and probably caused people there to wonder whether a person, if he joined the church after a general manumission, might not jeopardize his status by abandoning the church. The idea that they were concerned emerges from a consideration of the precise wording of the mass manumission of the village which dates from about fifteen years after Jean's fight. In that manumission it is explicitly noted that the freedmen may "take or" (not a common phrasing) "put off" the clerical tonsure without affecting their personal freedom. It was not even to be supposed, in other words, that any condition adhered to those who took the tonsure.[4] If, as seems likely, a few recipients of freedom in the late thirteenth-century Sénonais chose to join the church under the power conferred by a general manumission, they did so with greater confidence that their potential apostasy would incur only spiritual censure not resumption of their servitude.[5]

The second and much more complex issue that Sénonais evidence illuminates on the legal limits of manumission and the complicating effects on the plans and behavior of freedmen involves marriage and its relation to status descent—and through status descent, on inheritance. Sometimes, especially in nonregional manumissions involving small numbers of families, there were no logical complications with regard to marriage and lineage that can be said to have tainted the grants. In 1224, for example, an entire family—adults, children, and heirs—achieved freedom from "every taille and *corvée* and every corporal servitude." Whatever they did thereafter may have messed up their lives, but there is no reason to think that they were troubled by the grant per se as it touched their inheritance rights.[6] Similarly, in 1277 the abbey of Saint-Remy of Sens in return for an annual tax of three shillings *parisis* freed Etienne dit Guigniez and his wife, Benoîte, both of whom were dependents of the abbey at Vareilles; it explicitly "manumitted, freed and quitted" their heirs "from every burden, service, and servitude."[7] Again, it is hard to imagine a problem since a married couple and their children, all of whom were dependents of Saint-Remy, were manumitted.

To be sure, manumissions could and sometimes did include provisions that restored mainmortability under circumstances in which a person voluntarily entered into a seigneurie or a personal relationship to which mainmort adhered as of right. The very fact that lords had to be careful about monitoring their freedmen on a point such as this shows nicely that there must have been disputes about it. The freedmen would have argued that once they had been delivered from mainmort they would always be quit of the disability. A recognition by the bishop of Auxerre in 1276 in which he insisted that he had not compromised the rights of other lords to impose the liability of mainmort on his freedmen if they should acquire goods in other mainmortable seigneuries shows clearly that the upper class was of a rather different mind.[8]

A more pressing issue, however, was what effect a manumission had on the children of out-marriages when only one parent was freed. This was a more pressing issue because in some manumissions where names are available it appears that about 20 percent of the married people affected were married to "foreigners," dependents of different lords from the manumitting lord. This has been shown by Maximilien Quantin to have been true among the residents of Soucy (over 330 people) manumitted by various lords in 1283,[9] and it is strongly suggested by all those conventions between lords to split the possessory rights over children of out-marriages: the abbot of Saint-Remy of Sens entered into such agreements with nobles of the region in 1276 involving 60 couples and at least 127 children.[10] It can be further confirmed by a brief analysis of the freedmen of Saint-Pierre-le-Vif of Sens.

Of the Saint-Pierre group (366), 31 refer to husbands or parents who, though not dead, were not enrolled under the final accord. These 31 divide into two unequal parts. A group of 26 wives and children, among them Claire Gaignart whom we encountered in the last chapter, obligated themselves to pay for their own manumission (that is, to contribute to the purchase price) because their fathers and husbands who should have assumed legal responsibility for this had not the legal capacity to do so.[11] They were dependents of other lords; so, the situations had originated as a result of out-marriages.[12] Given the number of family groups enumerated in the manumission, this translates into a very rough estimate of 20 percent of out-marriages among all marriages. The remaining five cases, all of which involve freed women, reveal that the husbands of these women obligated themselves to pay for their wives' manumission, although the men themselves were not freed by the act.[13] It follows that they were already free, since they could enter into this contract. We have before us, in other words, five mixed-marriages, a subject to which we shall return.

With the high proportion of out-marriages that the data point to, it was obviously a matter of widespread urgency to anticipate the problems that manumission might have on these unions and their offspring. No single lord, after all, by his own act freeing the heirs of his *homo de corpore*, could abrogate the rights of the lord of the spouse in some portion of those heirs. It follows that after any mass manumission or similar grant there must have been a flurry of negotiations between individual freedmen or newly enfranchised communities of freedmen and the lords of their spouses with the intention of purchasing those spouses' liberty and, therefore, securing their children's inheritance. The only exceptions might have been those in which the married couple was childless and no longer young enough to bear children.

We have already had some indication of this flurry of activity in the examples of freedmen in Sens who within one or two years after their manumission were obliged to accept responsibility for taxes in the city on their wives' property, once that property had lost its mainmortability upon the manumission of the wife.[14] Another pertinent example comes from somewhat earlier records. In 1223 Lord Dreu de Mello and the abbey of Saint-Remy of Sens made one of the classic conventions with regard to out-marriages in Villeneuve-la-Guyard. A contention had arisen over which lord should get the minor children and goods of a woman who had married for the second time. A compromise was worked out so that they divided the ownership of the family into two parts. But the specific case led to a general agreement, which presumably applied to all second marriages, that "if it should happen that the men of the abbot marry the women of Dreu or vice versa, the children born from such a union, along with all their goods, ought to be divided in half between the lords."[15] Then, some years later, in 1234, the abbey reached an agreement with a freedman named Alemannus, probably a freedman of Dreu, who was married to a rustic of the abbey in Villeneuve-la-Guyard. For the imposition of a five-shilling *provins* annual tax he secured his wife Florence's manumission and that of half of his children (born and unborn) that the abbey claimed, since obviously his own change of status had not affected its claim to its portion of his children. Failure to meet the obligation each year on time doubled the tax.[16]

It was on the issue of mixed-marriage that the fragility of the law or of custom was most manifest. The evidence comes from a mid-century court case, whose origin goes back many years to the problems of Robert dit Sergent and his wife, Marie. This couple had had two children, a son, Jobert, and a daughter, Sédile. Jobert, although he lived to adulthood, predeceased his parents and died unwed. They attempted to appropriate his goods but were stymied by the abbey of Saint-Remy. Regarding their attempt as an effort to undermine the abbey's personal lordship, Saint-Remy used the incident as the occasion to demand an admission of abject servility from Robert and Marie. In 1246, the year of these events, the two people acknowledged that they were and that their dead son had been dependent on the abbey and, therefore, subject to mainmort. They then withdrew their claim to Jobert's goods but received them from the abbey at its pleasure.[17]

At some unspecified date, their daughter, Sédile, married Roger de Pont-sur-Vanne, a free man, by whom she had two daughters, Ermengard and Adeline. A little before 1260 the girls' parents died, and they attempted to succeed to their parents' goods. Immediately Saint-Remy claimed the girls and implicitly the goods by the principle "partus sequitur ventrem" (the status of the child follows the womb) and argued, before the *bailli* of Sens, for the customary application of this principle in the Sénonais. The problem could only have arisen in the first place because of Ermengard and Adeline's father's failure to purchase his wife's delivery from mainmort; that Sédile was in dependency to Saint-Remy was not disputed. The case became a *cause célèbre* and was appealed to the Parlement of Paris. In 1260 the masters of the king's court ruled that Saint-Remy had not proved anything to their satisfaction and so could have nothing of the girls' patrimony.[18]

This decision, which pitted the king against Sénonais lords, seems to have thrown some seigneurs into a frenzy of activity. Of course, there was some evidence in recent Sénonais history that status descended through the mother. In the manumission of dependents of Saint-Pierre-le-Vif, only three years before Parlement's decision, five free men had purchased their wives' manumission, presumably because they thought that their failure to do so would jeopardize the inheritance rights of their children. Interestingly, the interpretation of the Saint-Pierre evidence has a complication. The five women involved, who had been manumitted in 1257, may have been among those people who did not believe, or who said that they did not believe, that they were dependents of Saint-Pierre. The manumission of 1257 was to them merely a recognition of their existing liberty. When they had made their marriages to free men, they would not have considered them mixed-marriages at all. It is hard to imagine, for example, that Bernard de La Chapelle, one of the husbands involved here and a minor nobleman, had married a woman whose status would jeopardize his dignity and the inheritance rights of his children.[19] However, if he and the other husbands in these cases had knowingly married women under severe jural disabilities or if they were unsure of being able to defeat Saint-Pierre's claim that their wives were mainmortable, it made sense to buy their way out of the mess, since in some quarters at least it was being asserted that the dependency of a mother gave a lord rights in the children, irrespective of the status of the father. Three years later, in the aftermath of the Ermengard-Adeline court case, they might well have behaved differently.

The potential for resistance noted in the last sentence explains, I think, a few important documents from 1260 in which the archbishop of Sens and the cathedral chapter put pressure on people to declare that their status depended on that of their mothers. In June a curious arrangement with certain bourgeois insisted that the parties to a marriage between a man wholly dependent on the archbishop and a woman half dependent on the king through her father and half dependent on the archbishop through her mother would be obliged to pay the archbishop five shillings a year. Even if the husband died, the widow remained obligated for half of this sum, a fact that suggests the preponderant strength of claims through the mother.[20] In the very next month Girard dit Barrauz acknowledged that he could not move freely to Villeneuve-le-Roi "because he was one half the man, *ex parte matris*, of the dean and chapter" of the cathedral of Sens.[21]

The formal legal records give us little information about the underside of these agreements, but what they do provide is invaluable. The Sénonais prelates apparently made an extraordinary effort to get some firm testimony of status descent, possibly conceding material advantages they might not otherwise have conceded. To obtain the first agreement they brought a lengthy dispute to a quick conclusion, and in a stripping away of euphemism not unknown from time to time, confessed that they agreed to refrain from "demanding, asking or indeed extorting anything" beyond that precisely granted to them—almost irrefutable evidence of concessions on their part.[22] The other record refers rather more cryptically to Girard dit Barrauz's having been "led by wicked counsel" to go live where he wanted as the son of a free father, an allusion just possibly to the influence of those who were defending the interests of Ermengard and Adeline that year. He was, however, induced "by the advice of good men" to return and even to pay a fine.[23] The record of his capitulation was filed with evidence that the cathedral was collecting on the "conditionality" of manumission to the clergy.[24]

Recognitions such as these could be alleged in future court cases whenever challenges were raised against the claims of lords to the children of mixed-marriages in which the dependent partner was female. The lords of the Sénonais did not want to be taunted again by the judges of the king's court because they could prove nothing and therefore could secure no rights to anything. Two consequences flowed from the cluster of incidents treated here: (1) The public success of the archbishop and cathedral to press their view of status descent probably meant that existing methods of trying to assure free status in the face of a mother's jural disability, such as through the bearing of children outside the seigneurie of the mother's lord, would wane or people would less confidently assert that such methods conferred freedom. (2) The multiplier effect of a mass manumission was reconfirmed, since there was no viable alternative to protect inheritance rights of future children except through recently manumitted males (parties to out-marriages) purchasing the manumission of their still dependent wives.

What is fascinating and important to mention is the fact that parties might reach agreements wherein lords, about to manumit their own dependents, stipulated that they would try to induce other lords whose dependents had intermarried with theirs to be-

stow (sell) manumission as well. This was the only way to abrogate the agreements about division of seisin in children of out-
marriages without compromising the principle of status descent
that Sénonais lords were favoring. Such an arrangement was
easier to reach if the number of lords who had to get involved was
small and if their interests were more or less in tandem. This
seems to have been true in the manumission of Soucy in 1283.
During the archepiscopate of Gilles Cornu the Younger, the dean
and chapter of the cathedral of Sens reached an agreement with
the treasurer of the church, Alberic Cornu, to manumit their re-
spective *homines et femine de corpore* in the village; this superceded,
as we would expect, an earlier convention about the division of
seisin in the children of out-marriages.[25] The manumission informs us that the new agreement took place "at the prayer and
request of the said dean and chapter *and of their men*" of Soucy
(my emphasis). It then explicitly reveals the reason: so that children and future children of these people would be "manumitted
and acquitted . . . in perpetuity," without residual complications.[26]

Not enough attention has been paid to the intensity or nature of
the concern that dependents felt over these arrangements. To be
sure, they desired to protect the transmission of their property;
and free status assured, or seemed to assure, *integral* transmission
without the debasing inheritance tax (mainmort). But their interest was not founded merely on the rather bloodless desire for tax
immunity or even on a disembodied, idealized concern for the
economic viability of the lineage, albeit one supposes that, as with
the nobility, these sorts of considerations played a role in familial
strategies.[27] Instead, their principal concern arose out of something rather more than pecuniary considerations and rather less
than ponderings on their lineage: their hopes were vague and inflated, but they concentrated on their living children and grandchildren, not on the remote offspring of future generations. This
may seem too obvious a conclusion to state, but medieval historians by studying documents that have survived in abundance,

namely, those that originate in pecuniary questions, tend to transform the past into a succession of squabbles over financial well-being. Or else, they balance this picture with the platitudes of ecclesiastics, who said, "all men by natural law ought to enjoy the privilege of freedom" or who claimed that the church, the lord *par excellence*, "as the mother of all the faithful should not only grant the privilege of freedom but protect and defend what has been granted by others."[28] The real question is not whether lower-class people acquiesced in these sentiments, so often repeated.[29] Of course, they did: one of the battle-cries of peasant rebels and of the defrocked priests that sometimes led them was freedom for all people,[30] as good an indication that there was a mystique to freedom at such times as we are likely to require.[31] But revolutionary moments are often given over to sloganeering, whose relevance to "ordinary" daily life may be doubted. If the desire for freedom really touched the hearts of people in the thirteenth century, if it meant more than tax relief, how did they show it? It is not enough, finally, to say that they paid a great deal for it. People can be induced to pay enormous sums for the purest pecuniary advantages.

Some admittedly problematic Sénonais evidence may illuminate some of these matters outside the explosive and distorting context of rebellion and will, I think, give an added dimension to freedmen's concern with heirship—specifically, a less detached, more human, and, therefore, more historically accurate quality. I have analyzed closely the personal naming patterns of the group of men and women manumitted in 1257 who were isolated in the case study and have conjectured why the first name Félis (Felisius) or its feminine form Félise (Felisia) appears so often in the manumission: Félis Baillot, Félis Biauvilain, Félise Bourgignonne, Félis Cartaux, Félise Cate, Félis Chastri, Félis Claviger, Félis Doriau, and others. Only three other names, with their feminine forms (when they are in use), occur more often: Jean, Pierre, and Etienne.[32] That Félis should come next, exceeding otherwise common names like Jacques, Thomas, Eudes, Gilles, Thibaut, seemed odd.[33]

Further investigation revealed that not all social groups were quite so attached to the name Félis. One seeks it not in vain but with little success, for instance, in the thirteenth-century rolls of the city of Sens, at least outside the parishes inhabited in large measure by people under severe jural disabilities.[34] Contemporary lists, mostly of males—nobles, clerics, and persons born free—in the Sénonais, rarely include a Félis among them. There was a chaplain of the royal chapel of Sens with the name.[35] And there are doubtless other examples.[36] But the rarity of the name except among those of debased status is striking to anyone who is familiar with the manuscripts. Of the hundreds of masculine names in the records of mass manumissions in the Sénonais in the thirteenth century, however, a sizable proportion will always consist of *Felisii*. Unfortunately, this fact is not always easily shown since most published manumissions do not print the names.[37] This editorial convention is particularly distressing when a manumission exists in which female names predominate (possibly a consequence of the manumitting of female spouses in out-marriages). It is only from manuscripts that one comes to the realization that Félise was probably the most common feminine name in the entire region among women who were "mainmortable."[38]

How does one explain the prominence of Félis in general, that is, independent of its apparent restriction to a single social group? Reference to the local cult of Saint Felix or a saint with a similar name (Felicitas, Felicianus, Felicissimus, Felicula all appear conventionally on calendars in Sénonais churches) will suffice.[39] An active cult of Saint Felix flourished in the Sénonais; and he and his relics were honored on 14 January in the churches.[40] But if it is easy to explain why Félis in general was an acceptable baptismal name, its evident restriction to a distinct social category remains problematic. I have no faith in the only argument that seems to have been made, to wit, that the name, which means happy, expresses a point of view, encapsulated in the phrase "Gallic verve."[41] This would be the same sort of Gallic verve that is said to explain name choices like Chignart (Grumbler), Lepus (Hare), and Angoisseus (Anguished), but all of these are last names or nicknames and may at some remote time have been attached to distinguish the bearer of a rather ordinary baptismal name. Félis was obviously different.

No immediate explanation leaps to the mind for the restriction of Félis to a distinct social category; yet there are other examples of group specific naming in medieval France and elsewhere to which it can be compared: the restriction of Philip and Louis to the royal family and converted Jews; the restriction of the name Pleasant to the servile population of American slaves seven centuries later and a continent removed.[42] Pursuing the latter comparison, we would find that Pleasant was the third most popular name among descriptive, episodic, and occupational first names among male slaves, while its incidence among free blacks (many of whom had been born slaves) was decidedly less though not as low as among free whites where the name was nearly nonexistent.

The interesting phenomenon is not, however, that a name is social group specific, but under what pressures it loses that status. Félis, for example, ceased to be given as a baptismal name to the children and grandchildren of those manumitted in 1257. The correlation can hardly be coincidental, but before an explanation is offered, a few words need to be directed toward the evidence for the erosion of the name. Obviously, in the absence of registries of birth, it cannot be entirely conclusive. What is meant by the use of the word *erosion* is that for several families that had members named Félis (families where we might have expected the name to reappear) the name is not employed in subsequent generations. Félis Baillot bestowed the names of Gilles and Marie on his children.[43] Félis Charpentier, who comported himself as a free man, named his children Douce, Gui, and Pierre.[44] No subsequent members of the Bourgignon family bore the name Félis despite the fact that a Félise Bourgignonne was manumitted in 1257.[45] But aside from examples, the really powerful proof of the hypothesis comes from the fact that not one of the people manumitted whose successors in tenancy can be identified from charters or obituary books had a single heir named Félis or Félise.[46]

The explanation for this development—assuming it is not a ghost produced by the sketchy evidence—is the simple one: people realized that the name smacked of servitude which was vile (*vilibus servitutibus et costumis*).[47] They consciously abandoned it after manumission. A monk writing up an obit about the same time remarked on the process (though not with regard to our group of people). He called attention to Raoul Villein of Sens who had abandoned his servile-sounding last name when he referred to a few houses that "had belonged to the late Raoul called formerly the villein."[48] Perhaps I am misinterpreting his prose and he refers to a change of status rather than a change of name. This much can be said for my interpretation: it would not have been unusual in the Sénonais to have borne the name Villein, either as a first name (an early thirteenth-century member of the Dallemant family was named Villein Dallemant) or as a last name (compare Félis Biauvilain, modern French Beauvilain).[49] In other words, Raoul could have borne the name Villein; and if he did, he changed it.

Regardless of how we interpret the reference to Raoul, we are probably on solid ground in identifying and explaining the shift away from Félis, because such general shifts have been observed in many other circumstances. To begin with, we can fruitfully invoke the comparison with the slave name Pleasant. The desire of American blacks to change names after their emancipation and the distinct modifications in naming patterns for post-emancipation births, especially the erosion of the name Pleasant, are in fact well attested.[50] Richard Tomasson has shown how naming patterns were revolutionized in medieval Iceland, to give an illustration closer in time to the shift on Félis, after the coming of Christianity in the eleventh century as names evoking the pagan gods were eroded.[51] To be cautious, we should remind ourselves that baptizing bishops in Iceland probably refused to accept pagan-sounding names at the font, so that to measure the change in naming is partly to conflate clerical rigor (suppression), sponsors' hesitancy to suggest pagan-sounding names, and whatever real changes there were in popular mentality. Nonetheless, a last example may be adduced from similar changes in naming practice among the Imbonggu of New Guinea, the favorite geographical comparison it seems for many scholars. There these changing practices reflect largely noncoercive variations in status and emotional commitment, especially religious.[52]

We may never have vivid and certain knowledge of the emotional component of what ordinary people in the European Middle Ages expected from manumission. The best perhaps that we can accomplish is the sort of frankly imaginative reconstruction that the great H. S. Bennett gave us of life on an English manor.[53] Yet, the discussion of naming has been intended as a way to get at emotional states outside of the extreme case of rebellion. It is one way to demonstrate that rustics' concern with heirship transcended mere considerations of property and gave an ardor even to the nonviolent achievement of freedom. All of this reconfirms a point made at the beginning of the study: if we do not look for social struggle and the nexus of emotions that underlay the apparently placid and intensely "legalized" surface of thirteenth-century life, we are not likely ever to paint a trustworthy picture of human relations in the past.

Epilogue

The context within which social and legal problems of status were addressed in the thirteenth century changed decisively as the period drew to a close. The desire for freedom remained profound; yet, the numerous examples (and experiences) of manumission, by then stretching beyond the memory of living men, had provided the strongest possible evidence to lords that a mere grant of freedom did not compromise or prejudice claims to fundamental economic rights. The lords' refrain, increasingly heard but not really new, was that many lucrative rights inhered in *land*lordship.[1] Lords throughout northern France, chief among them the kings, exploited this truth and, when they could, used the manumissions as vehicles to affirm or reaffirm their landlordly rights.[2]

Nevertheless, the qualifier, "when they could," should serve as a warning against oversimplification. A king had options that other seigneurs did not enjoy. And furthermore, powerfully persuasive as the historical record in favor of manumission was, there were countervailing tendencies. Increasing indebtedness of the peasantry in the last decades of the century, to give one example, complicated negotiations about purchase prices.[3] This indebted-

97

ness arose largely out of the widespread stagnation of the economy, as early as 1250 in some regions, followed by a mild but persistent depression from about 1285 on.[4] Lords indeed were responding to the same pressures: many seem systematically and fervently to have interpreted the obligations of their tenants to them more strictly, to impose what in hindsight has sometimes been called "a new serfdom," thus encouraging new demands for freedom—demands that shaded into rebellion.[5]

These observations explain why the thirteenth-century manumissions, on the whole, form a coherent group of acts and why they must be distinguished from the "agreements" that capped the frequently more violent social struggles of the fourteenth century.[6] Recall, for example, the problem of inflation and lord's income.[7] We have seen that the thirteenth-century saw a steady erosion of the value of the French pound. But although steady, it was slow. Inherently there was time to adjust to the situation: conscious, sober measures—often very slow measures, like buying up of subleases—were part of the response.[8] Such an approach must have appeared pointless during, say, the inflationary leaps incident to the currency manipulations of Philip the Fair, and so it was abandoned in favor of decisive political action.[9]

So, too, the disruptive influences of war and plague in the fourteenth and early fifteenth centuries changed the rules of the game in ways we are only just beginning to penetrate. As the criminal records from this period are more thoroughly searched they show us the disruptors and the disruptions of life with almost as much lurid enthusiasm and in far more detail than even the well-known chroniclers' reports.[10] As rentbooks are studied with greater intensity, they reveal, predictably, the mid-fourteenth century as a period of wide-ranging renegotiation of rents and conditions of tenure and the sharpening of differences of wealth within village communities, with all of the unfortunate consequences that the latter brings.[11] In the midst of this disruption (indeed, largely because of it) there continued to flourish what can only be called an atavistic attachment on the part of lords to the servile regime of the previous century. This was their idealized view of the past: we have seen that in fact the relation of bondman to lord was frequently problematic in the thirteenth century. Still, they yearned for a return to the good old days of Saint Louis— when the coinage was sound and people knew their proper place.[12]

The Sénonais, like other regions in northern France, suffered this transformation in human relations and attitudes. Indebtedness and corruption led to the suppression of the commune of Sens in 1317.[13] Attacks of the plague in 1349 and again in 1351 laid families and estates low.[14] Renegotiation of rents and conditions of tenure from the late thirteenth through the mid-fourteenth century, as evidenced by early modern rent books and inventories which frequently trace holdings only as far back as this "formative" period, heralded a veritable revolution in tenancy.[15] The depredations of the Hundred Years' War (1338–1453) upset the superficial equilibrium of life even in the city of Sens itself.[16] Acts of terrorism laid bare the fragility of social relations. One episode can stand for many: the early fifteenth century witnessed the dreaded activities of a criminal known by the ominous sobriquet of "The Digger." He was a thief, a murderer, and an arsonist. A quaint story tells how he "cremated" (nice word) some of the property of the abbey of Saint-Colombe of Sens at Reigny.[17]

All of these facts make the later history of relations between seigneurs and tenants in the Sénonais potentially more exciting for those willing to immerse themselves in the mass of manuscript materials than the history of those relations in the thirteenth century. If the clue to those relations can no longer be the highly formal, "legalized" process and act of manumission with its garland of fiscal and juridical complications, the central substantive issue, I suggest, remains essentially the same: the meaning and limits of freedom, that mystically vague notion embodied in a status that men and women in the thirteenth century paid dearly for; that men and women in the fourteenth century and since have often purchased with their lives.

Notes

Manuscripts held by the Archives Départementales, the Archives Nationales, and the Bibliothèques Municipales are identified by bundle numbers; individual manuscripts are sufficiently identified in the notes. The following abbreviations have been used.

AD: Archives Départementales
AN: Archives Nationales
BM: Bibliothèque Municipale
SAAube: Société Académique de l'Aube
SASens: Société Archéologique de Sens
SHYonne: Société des Sciences Historiques et Naturelles de l'Yonne

CHAPTER I
Historiography and Sources

1. Topography in general: *Dictionnaire topographique: Yonne*, pp. iv–v. On the Othe: *Dictionnaire topographique: Aube*, pp. ii, ix; *Histoire de la France rurale*, 1:233. On the recluses, see Dauphin, "Vallée de Valprofonde," p. 9; Cousin, "Anciens

ermites et ermitages," part 1, pp. 103, 150, and part 2, p. 64. On the wolves: *HF* 21:233 (bounties paid, 1230s); Blin, procès-verbaux (7 July 1935), *SHYonne: Bulletin*, 90 (1935): xxxii; Moreau, "Loups dans l'Yonne," pp. 177–91.

2. *Dictionnaire topographique: Yonne*, préface. Some of the medieval bridges on the tributaries and the two main rivers are noticed in Quantin, "Histoire de la rivière d'Yonne," pp. 439–40, 442; cf. Estienne, *Guide des chemins de France de 1553*, 1:308 n.175; and in the very names of the medieval towns: Pont-sur-Vanne, Pont(s)-sur-Yonne.

3. Fishing rights: AD: Yonne, F 441, 474. Tolls: Lecoy de La Marche, "Coutumes et péages," pp. 277–81; Monceaux, "Coutumes et péages," pp. 303–48; Quantin, "Histoire de la rivière d'Yonne," pp. 415–16, 476.

4. *HF* 21:273–74. Jordan, *Louis IX*, p. 94 n.95.

5. Quantin and Boucheron, "Mémoire sur les voies romaines," pp. 1–72 (with an excellent end map); *Dictionnaire topographique: Yonne*, p. vii; Pignaud-Péguet, *Histoire illustrée: Yonne*, p. 957; Hubert, "Frontière occidentale du comté de Champagne," map p. 13; Blin, "Recherches sur un chemin médiéval de l'Yonne à la Loire," map p. 30; Carré, "Voies romaines," pp. 1–15; "Toponomastique de la région de Sens," p. 249; and the map appended to Hugues, *Routes de Seine-et-Marne avant 1789*.

6. Renaissance roads: Estienne, *Guide des chemins de France de 1553*, 1:68, 70–71, 73. Medieval backroads: Mignardot, "Monographie de Michery," pp. 55–60.

7. *Dictionnaire topographique: Aube*, pp. 52, 68, 75, 88, 107; "Toponomastique de la région de Sens," pp. 247–84.

8. Prou, *Coutumes de Lorris*, pp. 108, 112–14, 120–22. Prou's list, however, needs modification and supplementing: his reference for the village of Gisy is incorrect (cf. Quantin, *Recueil de pièces*, no. 573); his location of Lixy should read "Canton, Pont-sur-Yonne" not "Canton, Chéroy." Add to his list: Champigny, Villeblevin, Villeneuve-la-Guyard and Villeneuve-l'Archevêque (Quantin, *Recueil de pièces*, no. 573).

9. Yver, *Egalité entre héritiers*, juridical end map (based on Klimrath, *Travaux sur l'histoire du droit français*); the map referred to, however, should show the Auxerrois as part of the zone (see the *errata et addenda* of Yver).

10. Jordan, *Louis IX*, pp. 51–64, 153–54 n.108; Laurent, "Bailliage de Sens," pp. 319–49.

11. *Dictionnaire topographique: Aube*, pp. xxvii, 24, 112.

12. Jordan, *Louis IX*, pp. 42–43. On Champenois pressures on the neighboring Auxerrois, cf. Sassier, *Recherches*, pp. 197–217.

13. Lalore, "Documents . . . des anciens seigneurs de Traînel"; Defer, "Histoire de Traînel."

14. Arbois de Jubainville, *Histoire des ducs et comtes de Champagne*, 5:250; Pissier, "Etudes historiques sur Dixmont," pp. 14–15, 252–53.

15. Aufauvre, *Nogent-sur-Seine*, pp. 32–60.

16. *Olim*, 1:343–47 xiv. Pissier, "Frontières," pp. 105–15.

17. Jurisdictional squabbles: BM: Sens, MS 44, pp. 171–72. The *rattache-*

ment: Delaborde, *Jean de Joinville*, p. 140. Administrative integrity of Sens: Laurent, "Bailliage de Sens."

18. Hubert, "Frontière," map p. 8.

19. Quesvers, *Note sur quelques paroisses*, pp. 14–15; *Dictionnaire topographique: Seine-et-Marne*, p. iii.

20. Cf., for example, the holdings of the Traînel (above n. 13) and of the king: *Olim*, 1:160–61 vi; Brissot, "Notice sur Villeneuve-le-Roi," pp. 129–45; Aufauvre, *Nogent-sur-Seine*, pp. 32–60.

21. For the holdings of the cathedral: AD: Yonne, G 940, 941, 1247, 1282, 1310, 1314, 1315, 1328, 1330, 1351, 1389, 1390, 1421, 1485; *Olim*, 1:160–61 iv. For the holdings of Saint-Pierre: AD: Yonne, H 211, 212, 225, 227; *Livre des revenus*, passim; "Toponomastique de la région de Sens," p. 267; Horson, *Recherches historiques sur Pont-sur-Yonne*.

22. AD: Yonne, H 265, 284–85, 287, 297, 301, 306, 313, 320.

23. For Sainte-Colombe: AD: Yonne, H 5, 12, 97, 105, 108, 111; for Saint-Jean: H 376, 408, 415, 418, 429, 430; for Valuisant: H 709, 711, 716, 786, 787; for La Cour: H 787–808. Good studies, summarizing the landholding records of various houses, are the following: Brullée, "Notice sur . . . Notre-Dame de la Pommeraye," pp. 82–111; Salomon, "Histoire de l'abbaye des Escharlis," pp. 387–450; Régnier, "Histoire de l'abbaye des Escharlis," pp. 221–346; Pissier, "L'Abbaye Notre-Dame de Dilo," pp. 31–148; Roy, "Couvent des Dominicains de Sens," pp. 99–221; Carlier, "Popelin de Sens," pp. 54–67.

24. *Recueil des statuts*, p. 61, on the *pagus Senonensis*.

25. As one approaches the Sénonais today, one encounters signs still reading: "Découvrez / le pays sénonais— / harmonie / équilibrium." Nowadays the idea is to distinguish the Sénonais from hectic Paris.

26. Quantin, "Recherches sur le tiers-état," passim.

27. Full references to all of the works to be mentioned in the following historiographic review are provided in the bibliography at the end of the book.

28. Cf. the harsh criticisms of Razi, "The Toronto School's Reconstitution of Medieval Society," pp. 141–57; and his "Struggles Between the Abbots of Halesowen and Their Tenants," pp. 151–67.

29. Records such as these are scattered through the archives or published sources. In this book they are exploited largely for the case study in part 2.

30. Cf. Quantin, "Recherches sur le tiers-état," passim.

31. For an example of a bundle of such charters detailing realty transactions around Pont-sur-Yonne, see AD: Yonne, H 218. On the position of *officialis*: Fournier, *Officialités*.

32. AN: J 261 no. 13. Jordan, "Communal Administration," pp. 292–313.

33. Turlan, *Commune et le corps de ville de Sens*, p. 55 n.2.

34. AD: Yonne, H 51, MS 3 (with imperfect transcriptions MS 4 and G 54bis, MS 25); G 54bis, MS 27; Quantin, *Recueil de pièces*, no. 133; Maillard and Berruyer, "Rapports . . . dans l'archidiaconé de Sens," p. 123.

35. AD: Nièvre, 32 H 7 (ancien H 62), document marked on reverse "H 69 no. 2."

36. Inventory of Claude Laurent, *greffier*, AD: Yonne, G 726. Existing cartulary, published by Chartraire, *Cartulaire du Chapitre de Sens*.

37. *Chronique* of Geoffroy de Courlon. On the chronicle tradition in Sens, see Challe, "Chroniquers sénonais du moyen-âge," and Bautier and Gilles, *Chronique*, preface.

38. The discussion in the text is based on careful scrutiny of all the surviving thirteenth- and fourteenth-century Sénonais obituary books and the complementary rent books against which their information must be set, including the published versions of the so-called *Livre de revenus* of the abbey of Saint-Pierre-le-Vif, its published *Kalendarium*, and its unpublished rent lists (AD: Yonne, H 181, 215), obituary (BM: Auxerre, MS 214 [ancien 181]) and *Ceremoniale* (BM: Sens, MS 24). Among the records of the abbey of Saint-Remy of Sens, besides published fragments of its obituary records, see the rent book in AD: Yonne, H 306. For the Popelin (a hospital of Sens): AD: Yonne, H supp. 3760, 3761. For the abbey of Sainte-Colombe of Sens: BM: Sens, MS 44. For the cathedral of Sens: BM: Sens, MS 45. For other scholarly discussions of these sorts of records, see Huyghebaert, *Documents nécrologiques*; Lemaître, "Obituaires français," and now his *Répertoire des documents nécrologiques français*. Barbara Harvey, *Westminster Abbey*, Appendix II, has a good discussion of the use of similar English sources.

39. A few thirteenth-century testaments survive from the cathedral archives; see, for example, AD: Yonne, G 135.

CHAPTER 2
Status and Manumission in the Sénonais

1. Bloch, *Feudal Society*, 2:283–331.

2. See the masterful review essay of Hatcher, "English Serfdom and Villeinage," pp. 3–39; and the scintillating study by Smith, "Some Thoughts on 'Hereditary' and 'Proprietary' Rights," pp. 95–128. Also Dockès, *Medieval Slavery and Liberation*.

3. Evergates, *Feudal Society*, p. 13. Similar apprehensions, sometimes tantamount to a rejection of theory (cf. the criticisms of Hilton, "Towns in English Feudal Society," pp. 3–20), touch the words *feudalism, sovereignty, peasantry*, and, of course, *Middle Ages*; Brown, "Tyranny of a Construct"; Bisson, "Feudal Monarchy"; Benn, "Uses of Sovereignty"; Beckett, "Peasant"; Hilton, *English Peasantry*, p. 3; Burrows, "Unmaking 'the Middle Ages.'"

4. See *Histoire de la France rurale*, 1:475–82; cf. Hyams, *King, Lords and Peasants*, passim.

5. This point is discussed at greater length below, text to nn.42–43.

6. Quantin, "Recherches sur le tiers-état," pp. 22–24; *Histoire de la France rurale*, 1:493; Brissaud, *French Public Law*, p. 323; Jordan, "Mainmort."

7. Cf. a charter of 1188 referring to free burghers (*burgenses liberi*) under mainmort; Quantin, *Cartulaire général*, 2:385.

8. Bloch, *Feudal Society*, 1:250–51, 263; Bloch, "Liberté et servitude," pp. 296–99; Quantin, "Recherches sur le tiers-état," p. 15.

9. Bloch, "Liberté et servitude," pp. 297, 299–301; Hyams, *King, Lords and Peasants*, pp. 69–70.

10. Cf. Bloch, "Liberté et servitude," pp. 298–99; Quantin, "Recherches sur le tiers-état," p. 15.

11. Bloch, *Feudal Society*, 1:206; Bloch, "Liberté et servitude," p. 312; Nicholas, "Patterns of Social Mobility," p. 77; Brissaud, *French Public Law*, pp. 317–18 n.10.

12. Quantin, "Recherches sur le tiers-état," pp. 24–25; Bloch, "Liberté et servitude," pp. 301, 304–7, 316.

13. Quantin, "Recherches sur le tiers-état," p. 24.

14. Nicholas, "Patterns of Social Mobility," pp. 73–74.

15. Pissier, "Etudes historiques," pp. 14–15, 252–53.

16. Knackstedt, *Moskau*, pp. 169–72.

17. There are examples in AD: Yonne, H 176, from the early thirteenth century.

18. Since surnames became a fixture in northern French life only in the early thirteenth century (cf. Fossier, "Land, Castle, Money and Family," pp. 161, 163–64; Kosminsky, *Studies*, p. 229), Peter McClure's techniques on using surnames to establish migration patterns apply; see McClure, "Surnames," and his "Patterns of Migration," as well as Howell, "Late Medieval . . . City," pp. 9–10, for a positive evaluation of the techniques (whose details need not delay us here). I have used the parish lists in the town account of Sens (1260; AN: J 261 no. 13) to establish migration patterns. The parishes with large dependent populations were Saint-Savinian, Saint-Pierre, and Mâlay.

19. Evergates, *Feudal Society*, pp. 23–28; cf. Raftis, *Tenure and Mobility*, pp. 129–52.

20. Quantin, "Recherches sur le tiers-état," pp. 14–15.

21. Ibid., p. 25; Bloch, *Feudal Society*, 1:263; Bloch, "Liberté et servitude," p. 293; Brissaud, *French Public Law*, p. 320.

22. For the details that follow, see *Olim*, 1:117 ii. Also Quantin, "Recherches sur le tiers-état," p. 25; Brissaud, *French Public Law*, p. 317. Cf. Pollock and Maitland, *History of English Law*, 1:422–24; Hyams, *King, Lords and Peasants*, pp. 176–77.

23. Bloch, "Liberté et servitude," pp. 294–95. Cf. Brissaud, *French Public Law*, p. 317.

24. AD: Yonne, G 54bis MS 26; G 106 MSS 5, 6; G 729 (several manuscripts). Cf. Quantin, "Recherches sur le tiers-état," pp. 25, 261–62; also, Evergates, *Feudal Society*, pp. 22–23.

25. Quantin, "Recherches sur le tiers-état," p. 25.

26. *Olim*, 1:117 ii. Cf. Bloch, "Liberté et servitude," p. 298; Brissaud, *French Public Law*, pp. 318, 320; Nicholas, "Patterns of Social Mobility," p. 90.

27. Bloch, "Liberté et servitude," p. 326, esp. n.3.

28. Duby, *Rural Economy*, p. 243.

29. Quantin, "Recherches sur le tiers-état," p. 18; Bloch, *Feudal Society*, 1:263; Bloch, "Liberté et servitude," p. 325.

30. For evidence on what appear to be oblates (*pueri*; Quantin, *Cartulaire général*, vol. 2, no. ccx; Blaise, *Lexicon*, s.v. "puer") in Sénonais institutions in the twelfth century, see AD: Yonne, G 144 MS 1. On the church's changing attitude, see Boswell, "*Expositio* and *Oblatio*," pp. 17–23, 29.

31. On the matters treated in this paragraph, Duby, "Medieval Agriculture," pp. 188, 196, 205; Jordan, "Corvée," pp. 612–13.

32. Duby, "Medieval Agriculture," pp. 206–7; Bloch, *Feudal Society*, 1: 252–53; Bloch, "Liberté et servitude," pp. 301–4; Fossier, *Terre et les hommes*, 2:698–701.

33. Bloch, *Feudal Society*, 1:253.

34. AD: Yonne, H 176 MSS marked "Arces, 1220 mense Augusto"; and "de hominibus pro tallia de baissiaco," with tailles of 2 s. to 5 s.

35. As compared, say, to rural wages; see, e.g., AD: Yonne, G 940, recording annual wages to individual foresters of the cathedral of Sens in the thirteenth century ranging from 28 s. to 6 l.

36. For a discussion, largely correcting the older views of Bloch and Valous (*Temporel*, p. 111), see Lehoux, *Bourg Saint-Germain-des-Près*, pp. 9, 12–15; Fourquin, *Lordship and Feudalism*, pp. 174–75.

37. Bloch, *Feudal Society*, 1:264; Fourquin, *Lordship and Feudalism*, pp. 170, 172, 174; Berman, *Law and Revolution*, pp. 325–27.

38. On the position of these dependents before courts (royal and manorial), see, for example, Quantin, *Inventaire-sommaire des AD: Yonne, série H*, H. 32 (p. 40). More generally: Bloch, *Feudal Society*, 1:264–65; Nicholas, "Patterns of Social Mobility," pp. 78–79; Fossier, *Terre et les hommes*, 2:692–98; and, especially, Hyams, *King, Lords and Peasants*.

39. Cf. Berman, *Law and Revolution*, pp. 330–31.

40. Nicholas, "Patterns of Social Mobility," pp. 72–79; Hilton, *Bond Men Made Free*, pp. 83–85; Pirenne, *Economic and Social History*, p. 81.

41. Individual references to the charters enumerated here will be made in the course of the study. A number of the texts, sometimes poorly edited, are available in Quantin, *Recueil de pièces* (hereafter referred to as *Rdp*) and in his "Recherches sur le tiers-état," appendix. A great many examples are catalogued in the *Inventaire-sommaire* of series F (probably transcriptions and abstracts made by or for Quantin).

42. Bloch, "Liberté et servitude," p. 328; Quantin, "Recherches sur le tiers-état"; Dégouvenain, "Chartes de commune et d'affranchissement," pp. 54–112; Fourquin, *Lordship and Feudalism*, pp. 176–77.

43. *Dimittere* serves for the "enfranchisement" of the *burgenses* of Tonnerre from mainmort in 1211 (*Rdp*, no. 105). The "enfranchisement" of Sacy in 1214 "quitted" the bondmen of escheats (mainmort); *Rdp*, no. 136. *Remittere* is used in the "enfranchisement" of Chablis from mainmort in 1258; *Rdp*, no. 580. *Manumittere* is employed in what is called the "enfranchisement" of Saint-Aubin-Châteauneuf; *Rdp*, no. 628: "manumitted from the yoke of the condition of main-

mort." In the "manumission" of a *homo de corpore* in 1277, the operative phrase was "manumitted, freed and quitted"; *Rdp*, no. 695. Curiously, in neighboring Champagne the verb *manumittere* had different connotations; cf. Evergates, *Feudal Society*, pp. 28–30.

44. Bloch, *Rois et serfs*, pp. 26, 32, 45, 48–63, 66–68; Lehoux, *Bourg Saint-Germain-des-Près*, pp. 15, 30; Fossier, *Terre et les hommes*, 1:311, 2:692–98; Duby, "Medieval Agriculture," pp. 188, 196, 205, 208–9; and others.

45. This and the following discussion of rents has drawn fruitfully on the work of Valous, *Temporel*, pp. 95–104; Bloch, *Feudal Society*, 1:248–49. See also Sivéry, *Economie du royaume de France*, p. 132 (but cf. p. 117). Recent English work has been useful: Hockey, *Quarr Abbey*, pp. 67, 91; King, *Peterborough Abbey*, chaps. 5 and 6; Raban, *Estates*, chap. 4 (though she conflates land and rents).

46. Details on Sénonais landholding and rents will be given in parts 2 and 3.

47. Henneman, *Royal Taxation*, pp. 33, 44, 65, 76; Jordan, "Mortmain." Cf. Raban, *Mortmain*; Mate, "Property Investment," pp. 1–21.

48. Harvey, *Westminster Abbey*, p. 33.

49. Sivéry, "Mouvements de capitaux," p. 140.

50. AD: Yonne, H 37 MS 2, "Considerantes et attendentes redditus Thesauri monasterii nostri tenues esse et in multis pati defectum."

51. AD: Yonne, H 787, fol. 21, "redditus et proventus . . . sint tenues et exiles." Jordan, "La Cour."

52. Raban, *Estates*, p. 64; Dyer, *Lords and Peasants*, p. 56.

53. Valous, *Temporel*, pp. 104–23.

54. Pirenne, *Economic and Social History*, p. 65.

55. AD: Indre, H 181, dated 1332, with rubrics and notes such as "Hii sunt redditus qui possunt cresci et diminui" (fols. 1 v., 2 v., 3 v., 7 v., 8, 9, 12 v., 14, 15) and "Inquire" or "Inquire si fuerit plus" (fols. 9 v., 10, 11, 12, 14 v., 15, 16 v.).

56. BM: Sens, MS 45 (typical example at p. 317): "In cujus anniversario distribuimus quicquid provenit annis singulis ex locationibus domorum que fuerunt defuncti Radulfi dicti quondam villani empte a petro leonele et domorum que fuerunt Roselli cordubenarii et filiarum eius. empte a Guillelmo dicto gornaut clerico provenire."

57. AD: Nièvre, II. 1: "addens, statuens, atque volens idem Guido [donor] quod si contingeret quod ex fructibus, exitibus, et proventibus clausi et quarterii predictorum non possent precipi vel haberi dicti quadraginta solidi, defectus eorum de ipsius Guidonis vinee dicte de la perere fructibus et exitibus suppleatur."

58. See, for example, the careful records of the buying up of rents in the late thirteenth and early fourteenth centuries by the abbey of Noaillé of Poitiers; AD: Vienne, 1 H 5 liasse 3.

59. *Registres du Trésor*, vol. 1, nos. 308, 381, etc.

60. Ibid., no. 1016 recalls the prohibition. Evidence of its circumvention or at least of churches obtaining some of the properties includes the following: by the cathedral chapter of Soissons, the nunnery of Saint-Louis of Poissy, Saint-Cyr d'Issoudun, the abbey of Joyenval (ibid., nos. 317, 1427, 1909, 1947), by Saint-Hilaire de la Celle of Poitiers (AD: Vienne, 1 H 13 liasse 18).

61. For examples of subleasing in the thirteenth-century Sénonais, see AD: Yonne, H 787, fol. 41 r.; *Livre des revenus*, pp. 189, 191–92, 194, 204 (the fortunes of the Gaignart family); etc. The best discussions of subleasing, however, are based on English evidence: Pollock and Maitland, *History of English Law*, 1: 291–92 (with regard to free tenures); Raftis, *Tenure and Mobility*, pp. 74–81; Raftis, *Warboys*, pp. 167–68; DeWindt, *Land and People*, pp. 45–48; Harvey, *Westminster Abbey*, pp. 214, 307–11.

62. AD: Yonne, H 218, MSS entitled "1278 Censives et Coutumes de Beaumont" and "de costumis apud pontes pro Gaufrido abbate" (of 1280). Again the phenomenon has been documented in England as well: Hockey, *Quarr Abbey*, p. 91; King, *Peterborough Abbey*, pp. 121–22.

63. *Livre des reliques*, p. 82.

64. Valous, *Temporel*, pp. 166–67.

65. Raban, *Estates*, p. 18; Harvey, *Westminster Abbey*, p. 84.

66. AD: Yonne, H 403, internal packet marked, "Domaine, Cézy": "debitis maximis et urgentibus oneratum"; "debita de die in diem currerent ad usuram"; "dictum monasterium destruetur voragine usurarum." Further on monastic debt and usury, see, for France, Valous, *Temporel*, pp. 145–53; for England, Bowers, "From Rolls to Riches," p. 69.

67. Jordan, "La Cour," and below, part 2.

68. *Rdp*, no. 561 n.1.

69. Duby, "Medieval Agriculture," p. 208; Duby, *Rural Economy*, p. 243; Hilton, *Bond Men Made Free*, pp. 83–85; Lehoux, *Bourg Saint-Germain-des-Près*, p. 33.

70. Quantin, *Cartulaire général*, 2:483 (dated 1197), "pro relevanda ecclesie nostre obligatione debitorum urgentissima."

71. *Rdp*, no. 561, "urgente necessitate monasterii nostri"; also, "Recognoscimus eciam dictam pecunie summam in utilitate et commodum monasterii nostri esse versam." See, too, Lebeuf, *Mémoires*, vol. 2, "Recueil de monumens," pp. 56–58, nos. 124, 125.

72. *Rdp*, no. 1031. Richard, *Ducs de Bourgogne*, pp. 310–18, 362.

73. Dockès, *Medieval Slavery and Liberation*, pp. 174–96; Bloch, "Liberté et servitude," p. 346; Nicholas, "Patterns of Social Mobility," pp. 77–78; Berman, *Law and Revolution*, p. 330.

74. Quantin, *Cartulaire général*, 2:473–74, "pia consideratione ducti"; "manum mortuam . . . in perpetuum remiserunt. Ita quod in recompensationem hujus rei homines predicti ad furnum . . . per bannum, perpetuo coquere tenebuntur."

75. Quantin, "Recherches sur le tiers-état," pp. 29–35.

76. For example, Dockès, *Medieval Slavery and Liberation*, pp. 145–49.

77. For examples, see below, chap. 5, n.28.

78. To be sure, clerical opinion on whether even slavery was contrary to divine law had both its affirmers and deniers; Southern, *Making of the Middle Ages*, pp. 104–7.

79. *Rdp*, no. 105, "castellum meum de Tornodoro singulari amplectens amore."

80. Secular trends in the history of base dependency and its relationship to

rural lordship in general are treated in Hilton, *Decline of Serfdom*, and Fourquin, *Lordship and Feudalism*, pp. 203–39.

81. Richard, *Ducs de Bourgogne*, p. 339.

82. For example, "liberi sint et immunes foragio, stallagio, placitis generalibus, corveiis, toltis et talliis quibuscunque"; *Rdp*, no. 567. Hilton, *Decline of Serfdom*, p. 25; cf. Raban, *Mortmain*, p. 6.

CHAPTER 3
The Struggle for Freedom

1. On Geoffroy's connections, their careers and their influence on his career, see *Chronique*, p. 528; *Livre des reliques*, pp. xii, 83, and index s.v. "Norrais"; *GC*, 12:122, 129, 181. Gams, *Series episcoporum*, pp. 629–30; *Dictionnaire de biographie française*, 9:697–700; Bouvier, "Histoire de Saint-Pierre-le-Vif," p. 128; Baldwin, "Entourage de Philippe Auguste," pp. 67–70.

2. *Chronique*, p. 192; *Livre des reliques*, p. 7; Julliot, "Inventaire . . . 1660," p. 88. Bouvier, "Histoire de Saint-Pierre-le-Vif."

3. *Chronique*, pp. 504–8; *Livre des reliques*, p. 82. Bouvier, "Histoire de Saint-Pierre-le-Vif," p. 128.

4. *Livre des reliques*, p. 82; Gautier Cornu, "De susceptione coronae spineae Jesu Christi," *HF*, vol. 22. Larcher de Lavernade, *Histoire de la ville de Sens*, p. 89; Jordan, *Louis IX*, pp. 108, 193–95.

5. *Chronique*, p. 508; *Livre des reliques*, pp. 75, 86–87; BM: Auxerre, MS 213, p. 751. Bouvier, "Histoire de Saint-Pierre-le-Vif," p. 122.

6. AD: Yonne, H 253, MS marked on reverse "Ordonnances de L'Abbe."

7. Bautier and Gilles, *Chronique de Saint-Pierre-le-Vif de Sens, dite de Clarius*, pp. viii–xii, xlii, xlvi.

8. *Livre des reliques*, p. 84. Turlan, *Commune . . . de Sens*, p. 8; Bouvier, "Histoire de Saint-Pierre-le-Vif," pp. 126, 130.

9. AD: Yonne, F 412, internal bundle marked "Sens (St. Pierre le Vif) Rentes sur la cure de Neuilly," MSS "Charte 59," "Charte 62," and "Charte 63."

10. AD: Yonne, H 37, MS 2; *Livre des revenus*, pp. 247–48.

11. AD: Yonne H 674 MS 8. Further on the property holdings of Valuisant, H 709, 711, 716, 786–87.

12. AN: J 261 no. 13: "La vile devoit le roi . . . por samende." Actually it is not clear to me that this entry must refer to the old fine rather than to any of a set of new fines incurred in the mid-century (below n.14). Quantin (*Rdp*, no. 591 n.1) is the historian who has insisted on its relevance to the murder of Abbot Hébert.

13. AD: Yonne, H 51 MSS 2, 3, 4; G 54bis MSS 25, 27. Turlan, *Commune . . . de Sens*, pp. 26, 33; Bitton, *Sens*, p. 62; Duplès-Agier, "Notice sur une pièce trouvée au Trésor des Chartes," pp. 60–61.

14. *Olim*, 1:140–41 vii, 467 xv, 547–48 xii; *Livre des reliques*, p. 84. Bouvier, "Histoire de Saint-Pierre-le-Vif," p. 130. Infractions and disputes, however, continued: see AD: Yonne, H 51 MS 9 (dated 1268).

15. AD: Yonne, H 51 MS 7, "contencionis materia orta esset super hoc quod dicebamus homines prefatos et feminas esse de corpore homines et feminas . . . quod dicti homines et femine non confitebantur."

16. Cf. Hilton, *Decline of Serfdom*, p. 25.

17. AD: Yonne, H 51 MS 7, "in Villa Nova Regis . . . familia defuncti Hugonis de Arciis, familia defuncti Petri Ribaut eorum heredibus necnon et illis qui ab ipsis habuerunt originem."

18. Brissot, "Notice sur Villeneuve-le-Roi," pp. 129–45.

19. AD: Yonne, H 176 MS marked "Arces 1220 mense Augusto" (with imperfect paper transcription), "secundum usus vel consuetudines burgi Sancti-Petri." The imperfect transcription is no doubt Quantin's (cf. *Rdp*, no. 256). On Hugues's residence in the Bourg before 1220, see AD: Yonne, H 51 MS 5 (Quantin, *Cartulaire général*, 2:455–59).

20. *Livre des revenus*, pp. 154, 160.

21. Above, n.19, and AD: Yonne, H 51 MS 7.

22. AD: Yonne, H 176 MS "Recognitio Petri Ribaldi." The importance of the record was missed by Quantin (see his "Recherches sur le tiers-état," p. 14).

23. AD: Yonne, E 558 MS "1290, Evri: Charte d'Affranchissement" (a fifteenth- or sixteenth-century copy on paper).

24. *Rdp*, no. 261.

25. *Livre des revenus*, pp. 216, 226.

26. *Kalendarium*, p. 125, "jacet prope hostium camere thesaurii de cimiterio." The anniversary in this reference is 7 January because the scribe who copied the dates into this manuscript from a variety of existing books was a bad Latinist and a worse interpreter of dates. He seems to have had wrongheaded notions about what kalends, nones, ides, dominical letters, golden numbers, and even some Roman numerals were, but at least he was consistent in his errors. The "jacet" epitaph is also cited in Quesvers and Stein, *Inscriptions*, p. 568.

27. Dauphin, "Vallée de Valprofonde," p. 14.

28. Cf. Duby, "Medieval Agriculture," p. 208; Duby, *Rural Economy*, p. 243; Hilton, *Bond Men Made Free*, pp. 83–85; Lehoux, *Bourg Saint-Germain-des-Près*, p. 33. Even if other scholars ultimately discover higher charges, this would not invalidate the general point of the enormous cost of the manumission, given the number of people involved.

29. AD: Yonne, H 51 MS 7, "nonnulli hominum predictorum et feminarum sub dominio domini regis Francorum apud Villam Novam Regis se transtulerant et preter nostram voluntatem et licenciam in burgesia residenciam faciebant petentes ipsos homines et feminas a dominio rege compelli ad agnoscendum in predictis condicionem similem et reddi [MS: reddendi] sub dominio nostro."

30. *Rdp*, nos. 550, 597, with reference to a man "sub domino regis, apud Villam-Novam, quod facere non poterat nec debebat, ut dicebat, cum ipse esset homo ipsorum [dominorum]."

31. Dauphin, "Vallée de Valprofonde," p. 14; and below, nn.59–60.

32. AN: J 261 no. 13, "Johenne Lietarde" owed 10 s. p. "de la mise sire Gautier." The Gautier under whose mayoralty this levy was made served as the

head of the commune in 1239 (below, n.51). On the manumission he appears under the Latin name "Johannes Letardi." (All further references to the manumission are to AD: Yonne H 51 MS 7; the poorly edited version in *Rdp*, no. 567, cannot substitute because the names have not been published.)

33. Umberz xfoace. I do not understand the "x"; he is also listed in this record as Homberz Foace, Humberz Fovilte (a Latinizing form), Umberz Foace, Umbert Foace. The dates given in the text may be determined from the periods of administration of the various mayors under whom Humbert was assessed for communal levies. The identification of this Humbert with the Humbert who was the kinsman of La Clatelière and was "manumitted" in 1257 depends on the arrangement of the list of *emancipati* in the manumission and its collation with the geographical (parochial) arrangement of the fiscal account of Sens (AN: J 261 no. 13). Both Humberts occupy the same relative position.

34. AD: Yonne, H 225, MS marked with the date 1249 on reverse. On the manumission they appear, Johannes Mouflet, relicta Felisii Carpentarii, Petrus filius eius.

35. *Livre des revenus*, pp. 184–86; BM: Auxerre, MS 214, fols. 3 r., 17 r.

36. *Livre des revenus*, pp. 218, 224.

37. AN: J 261 no. 13; he was taxed at least as high as 27 s. in the *mise* of 1252.

38. *Livre des revenus*, pp. 184, 186, 235; *Kalendarium*, p. 130 (but for dating see n.26 above).

39. AD: Yonne, H 225, MS marked with the date 1249 on the reverse; the parties are "cives senonenses."

40. AD: Yonne, G 1359, internal packet "Paroisse St. Pierre le rond 1241," MS marked on reverse "littera de l. s. sitis super domo Johannis Mouflet."

41. AD: Yonne, G 1488, internal packet "Chapitre de Sens . . . Paroisse St Pregts . . . (1236)," MS marked on paper covering "1236."

42. *Livre des revenus*, p. 202.

43. Ibid., pp. 207, 213; AD: Yonne, H 225, MS marked 1249 on reverse.

44. In a curious entry of the late thirteenth-century obituary of the cathedral of Sens (BM: Sens, MS 45), the scribe went out of his way to mention that a house whose rent endowed an anniversary was the house in which Jean Mouflet had resided. The scribe had already given a precise location of the house; so, his reference to Mouflet was either redundant or emphatic. The use of the word *etiam* in the reference suggests the possibly emphatic character of the remark: "Obiit magister matheus de megreigniaco subdiaconus et noster canonicus. In cuius anniversario distribuimus triginta solidos par. percipiendos in molendinis des espeniaus iuxta Brayum. Et insuper quinquaginta solidos turonenses percipiendos super quadam domo sita in cordubenaria senonensis et inter quadam domum de vanna et domum quam tenet Johannes dictus Clericus draperius. In qua etiam Johannes dictus Mouflez cordubenarius moratur" (p. 314, 4 ides April). On the more general point about the leadership of popular movements by the relatively well-off, see Hilton, *Bond Men Made Free*, p. 96.

45. Manumission: Petrus Burgundus, Odo Burgundus. AN: J 261 no. 13 (municipal *mises*), Pierres (also Perreaus and Perriaus) li Borgoinz, Oedes li

Borgoinz. AD: Yonne, H 306, "Censier Abbaye St. Remy Sens," fol. 33 r.,
"Jacobus cordubenarius de porta sancti Antonii ii d. obole pro domibus que
fuerunt petri burgundi cordubenarii." Above Jacobus, subsequent tenants have
been enrolled in a later hand, "Odo cordubenarius et relicta Jacobi fratris sui de
porta sancti anthonii tenentur."

46. AN: J 261 no. 13, lists about thirty instances of people standing surety
for the debts of burghers. Gaudins Dallemant stood behind ten instances. No
other surety assumed the position more than twice. On procedures for sureties
and pledging, see Britton, *Community of the Vill*, pp. 103–9. An inventory of the
goods of another Dallemant, Adam, who served as precentor of the cathedral
of Sens in the early fourteenth century, valued his estate in excess of 1,000 l.;
Quantin, *Inventaire-sommaire des AD: Yonne: séries A-F*, s.v. "E. 99."

47. Etienne and Guillaume Dallemant purchased fiefs in the mid-thirteenth
century; *Rdp*, nos. 659, 664.

48. Guillaume Dallemant was guard of the fairs of Champagne in the count's
administration from 1276 to 1279, and he held the royal office of *bailli* of Troyes,
Meaux, and Provins from 1284 to 1286, that is, at the time of the *rattachement* of
Champagne to the royal domain. Subsequently he obtained the office of *bailli* of
Orléans. See Bautier, "Guillaume de Mussy," p. 72; *HF*, vol. 24, "Chronologie,"
pp. 47, 166; *Rdp*, no. 724; Benton, "Philip the Fair and the Jours of Troyes,"
pp. 313, 331. Maurice Roy, in error, makes Etienne the *bailli* of Orléans ("Couvent
des Dominicains de Sens," p. 110 n.3); but, although Etienne achieved something
like the status of elder statesman in the Sénonais (Guérin, "Enquête," p. 173), it
was because of other jobs that he had held. Another member of the family, Erard
Dallemant, served for a time as *bailli* of Amiens and Meaux; *HF*, vol. 24, "Chronologie," pp. 83, 168. He succeeded to part of Adam Dallemant's goods (above,
n.46).

49. See the rents listed in a contemporary *censier*; AD: Yonne, H 306, fols. 8
v., 9 r., 66 v.–67 r.

50. *Rdp*, no. 679.

51. The list of mayors that follows has been put together from various sources:
G=Giry, *Documents*, p. 101; H=d'Haucour, *Histoire de la ville de Sens*, p. 148;
J=AN: J 261 no. 13; Q=Quantin, *Histoire de la commune de Sens* (neither d'Haucour
nor Quantin always identified the sources; and I have not always been able to verify them).

Gilbert de Saint-Florentin	1209 (H,Q)
Thibaut du Moustier	1219 (H)
Gautier du Temple	1239 (J,Q)
Jacques Doustun	after 1239 but before 1249 (J)
Jeubert	after Jacques but before 1249 (J)
Jehan Le Peletier	1249 (H)
	1250 (H,J)
	1251 (H,J)
	1252 (H,J)

Etienne Dallemant	1254 (H,J)
	1255 (H,J)
Pierre Le Peletier	1258 (H,J,Q)
Etienne Dallemant	1259 (H,J,Q)
Nicolas de Villiers	1260 (H,J,Q)
	1262 (G)

52. For the information assembled here, see *Livre des revenus*, pp. 162, 164, 185–86, 208–9; *Rdp*, no. 664.

53. "Coram . . . Stephano Taste Saveur ballivo Senonensis"; on Etienne's career, see *HF*, vol. 24, "Chronologie," pp. 22, 38–39, 388.

54. Jordan, "Bailli," pp. 52–53.

55. On matters related to the king, see *HF*, 21:246–48. Also, Schramm, *König von Frankreich*, 1:223–33; Bouvier, "Histoire de Saint-Pierre-le-Vif," p. 127; Jordan, *Louis IX*, p. 110.

56. On Etienne's appointment, see Jordan, *Louis IX*, p. 145. Most of the records of the investigation of Sens and the Sénonais are lost; *HF*, vol. 24, "Préface," pp. 5, 6. On the crown's persistent interest in the social and political disputes in its towns, see *Olim*, 1:3 i, 6 iii, 15 xxvii, 74–75 xxviii, 183 xv, 191 vi, 314 xviii; and Jordan, "Communal Administration," pp. 306–9.

57. The reference is to negotiations taking place "coram nobili viro Gilone de Villamarchaz milite" and the *bailli* "ad hoc a domino rege specialiter destinatis," a point re-emphasized later in the manumission: "ad hec audienda a domino rege ut dictum est specialiter deputatis." Information on other aspects of Gilles's career may be gleaned from the wax tablets (running notes) of the royal chamberlain Jean Sarrasin, edited in *HF*, 21:332, 340–41, 359, 388.

58. On the church as finally constituted (a "monument of great proportions" according to Prou, with its altars and reliquaries completely outfitted with precious metals and gems and even its floor and windows renewed), see Prou, *Fouilles*, pp. 1, 3–5 nos. 1–10; Bouvier, "Histoire de Saint-Pierre-le-Vif," pp. 122–23, 130–31; Amé, *Carrelages*, part 1, pp. 106, 109–11, part 2, plates facing pp. 17–18.

59. For indications of the occasional isolated or individual grants or commendations in the Sénonais that had resulted in the possibility of manumitting scattered dependents, see *Rdp*, nos. 379, 436, 563; Lebeuf, *Mémoires*, vol. 2, "Recueil de monumens," p. 46, no. 97. On the difficulty of efficiently exploiting such people, cf. King, *Peterborough Abbey*, pp. 163–64; Raban, *Estates*, p. 57. AD: Yonne, H 214, various manuscripts of the thirteenth century refer to the abbey's dependents taillable on its estates. In the manumission, any dependents at Bray-sur-Seine are excepted ("excepto Braio").

60. See the texts cited in the preceding note. A legitimate but difficult question is the proportion of those ultimately covered by the manumission who were residents of Sens (or Villeneuve-sur-Yonne) and those whom I have characterized as scattered dependents. There are 366 names on the manumission of 1257. There exists a list, dated 1193, of the dependents of Saint-Pierre-le-Vif living in Sens (AD: Yonne, H 51 MS 5; Quentin, *Cartulaire général*, 2:455–59). On the list there

are 270 names, but there are some difficulties in direct comparison. Some of these 270 (or their descendants) emigrated. Hugues Le Roux d'Arces and his wife, for example, appear on the list of 1193 as residents of Sens, but as we know, they moved to Villeneuve-sur-Yonne around 1220. Others may have migrated elsewhere, but immigration partly or more than fully counterbalanced this phenomenon. However, if I take 270 as a rough indication of the size in Sens of the community of dependents of Saint-Pierre-le-Vif in the early thirteenth century and add a handful more for residents at Villeneuve-sur-Yonne, that would still leave about 75 or so people who were dependents of the abbey yet scattered here and there throughout the northern Sénonais. I should add that a decided overlap of surnames suggests rather stable residence patterns on the whole, a fact that gives me greater confidence in the conclusions in this note.

61. Manumission: ". . . a Secana usque Yoniam, a Braio usque Senones, excepto Braio, Mosterolium et usque ad Nogentum super Secanam et a Senonibus usque ad Villam Novam Regis et eciam in Villa Nova Regis."

62. *Livre des reliques*, pp. 83–84, "in burgo et in villis de Saligniaco, de Malleyo et usque ad fluvium Sequane."

63. AD: Yonne, H supplément 3761 (Hôtel-Dieu de Sens, Popelin II B 2; deposited in AD: Yonne in 1975); H 214, MS headed "Ce sont les terres, les vignes et li pre appertenanz a la maison de Paroy la quel est de Saint Pere le Vif de Senz"; H 313 MS marked "littere super rebus quas emimus apud Varellas a petro de henoto et eius uxore"; *Livre des revenus*, p. 168; etc.

64. This fact can still be appreciated by a visit to modern Sens. The old *ban* of Saint-Pierre-le-Vif, around the present rue Saint-Pierre-le-Vif, is on the very outskirts of the modern town. This was an area of intensive viticulture and is still an area of *rûs*, the irrigation ditches that date from the Middle Ages, and large vegetable gardens. On the *rûs* and the husbandry along them in the pre-modern period, see Julliot, "Notices," pp. 184–204; Perrin, "Histoire d'un cours d'eau," pp. 1–154; Perrin, "Rû de Mondereau," pp. 189–236.

65. *Chronique*, p. 528, "fuit fames et carum tempus."

66. Titow, *English Rural Society*, Appendix A, p. 97.

67. Sivéry, *Economie du royaume de France*, pp. 62, 90 (table 6), but the gaps in the French data base are well illustrated in the graphic presentation by Sivéry, pp. 70–110.

68. Titow, *English Rural Society*, Appendix A, pp. 97–98, Appendix B, pp. 100–102; Sayles, *Medieval Foundations*, p. 422; Hallam, "Climate," pp. 124–32.

69. AD: Yonne, H 225 MS marked with a faint "J" on the reverse, reference to property between one house and the "domum elemosine," 1262. See also H 169, a paper register of the eighteenth century detailing the *titres* of the Almonry (pp. 437–59), but they do not go back before 1291.

70. BM: Sens, MS 45.

71. AD: Yonne, H supplément 3771, III C 1 (dated March 1257 n.s.), "masculis liberis usque ad quartum decimum annum completum et filiabus usque ad duodecim annum completum in dicta parrochia decedentibus."

72. Quantin, "Histoire de la rivière d'Yonne," p. 479. On viticulture as a fa-

milial rather than a village collective enterprise, see *Histoire de la France rurale*, 1:459; Hilton, *Bond Men Made Free*, p. 32.

73. Dion, *Histoire de la vigne*, pp. 245–47; Rocher, "Bibliographie critique de l'histoire de la vigne," p. 23; Sivéry, *Economie du royaume de France*, pp. 16–17; *Histoire de la France rurale*, 1:466–67; Quantin, "Histoire de la rivière d'Yonne," pp. 349–498; Francis, *Wine Trade*, p. 15.

74. Hilton, *Bond Men Made Free*, p. 81.

75. Dion, *Histoire de la vigne*, pp. 246–47; Doehaerd, "Un Paradoxe géographique"; Hilton, *Bond Men Made Free*, p. 82.

76. On the husbandry of vines, see *Histoire de la France rurale*, 1:454–60.

77. For speculation on weather in northern France in 1250–59, see Sivéry, *Economie du royaume de France*, pp. 94–95; on England, see Sayles, *Medieval Foundations*, p. 422.

78. One must argue back from early and mid-fourteenth-century accounts; AD: Yonne, H 37 MS 10, H 178. The dispersed fragmentary records from which a detailed reconstruction of the abbey's finances in the thirteenth century might be made have never been adequately treated. Cf. Bouvier, "Histoire de Saint-Pierre-le-Vif," p. 141; and the reference to a lecture on this theme (never published) by Abbé Prunier, *BSA: Sens*, 10 (1872): 428 (Prunier's reputation, in any case, is not high; Lajon, "Sur les menhirs," pp. 239–42).

79. *Livre des reliques*, pp. 83–84.

80. Manumission: Theobaldus Munerius; Odo Malebeste, Johannes Malebeste, Felisius Malebeste.

81. *Livre des revenus*, pp. 216, 226.

82. AD: Yonne, H 214 MS "Hommes de Paroy, Volgre et Champlay," the list bearing the heading, "Ce sont cil qui durent largent de la charite." Possibly the archivist was confused, did not know that "charité" in the Middle Ages referred to alms or an alms house, and believed that the list must therefore relate to possessions of the abbey at La Charité (-sur-Loire). If so, this would explain his hesitancy in categorizing the list, because there is no other evidence of Saint-Pierre's possessions at the rather far-away town of La Charité. Two different archivists conjectured as to the dating of the sheet. One of them erroneously associated it with some other parchment and suggested 1396; the other rightly chose to date it to the thirteenth century.

83. *Livre des reliques*, pp. 83–84.

84. Manumission: "liberi sint et immunes foragio, stallagio, placitis generalibus, corveiis, toltis et talliis quibuscumque et de bonis suis omnibus et singulis possint disponere sicut liberi homines vendendo, donando, alienando et alias omnimode ordinando, prout sue sederit voluntati et se ac bona sua mobilia quecumque sint et ubicumque sint quandocumque placuerit sub alieno transferre dominio et domino et referre et redire si sibi placuerit vel viderint expedire, exceptis hereditagiis que tenent et tenebunt a nobis que non poterunt in manu mortua ponere vendere nec alienare. Cum extraneis poterunt maritare personis et se ac liberos suos ad clericatus ordinem vel religionis transferre."

85. AD: Yonne, H 167 MS marked "Inventaire des Tiltres . . . 1738," refer-

ring to "chartes du Roy Louys neuf qui Confirme La transaction faitte avec Les habitans Du Bourg St. pierre Maillot et Saligny qui ont payés Six milles Livres pour estre De Condition Libre avec permission D'aller Demeurer ou ils voudront." See also H 169, "Inventaire par ordre chronologique" (dated 1703), p. 3.

86. Manumission: "Prefati autem homines et femine manumissi ac heredes eorum commorantes in burgo nostro Sancti Petri Vivi Senonensis, in parrochia Sancti Saviniani et apud Malleotum Sancti Petri Vivi et in parrochia tenentur coquere ad furnos nostros et molere ad molendina nostra quia hactenus facere consueverunt licet sint liberi. . . . Et homines et femine commorantes apud Saligniacum tenentur coquere tantummodo et non molere ad furnum nostrum."

87. AD: Yonne, H 169, "Inventaire par ordre chronologique" (1703), p. 3, marginal note in a later hand, according to which, "La ditte charte [the manumission] prouve La banalité des Moulin de St. Pere et de Mailliot."

88. Manumission: "Et licet sint liberi dicti homines quamdiu erunt levantes et cubantes in Malleoto Sancti Petri et in parrochia ad reddendam singulis annis messonam maioris tenebuntur sicut antea faciebant. Et si recesserint de parrochia ad illam non tenebuntur."

89. Manumission: "Pastum vero domini archiepiscopi Senonensis seu procuracionem quadraginta solidorum debitam ut dicetur in crastino Pasche quando idem dominus archiepiscopus tunc celebrat in ecclesia Sancti Petri Vivi predicta non poterimus petere de cetero a dictis hominibus."

90. Manumission: "Item predicti homines et femine manumissi et eorum heredes quamdiu erunt manentes et commorantes in terris, villis seu justiciis nostris et in burgo nostro Sancti Petri Vivi erunt justiciabiles nostri sicut liberi homines. . . ."

91. Quantin, *Inventaire-sommaire des AD: Yonne—série H*, H. 32 (p. 40); Bouvier, "Histoire de Saint-Pierre-le-Vif," p. 21.

92. "Toponomastique de la région de Sens," p. 267; and above, n.90. Also Nicholas, "Patterns of Social Mobility," pp. 78–79; cf. Jordan, *Louis IX*, pp. 237–38.

93. Larcher de Lavernade, *Histoire de la ville de Sens*, pp. 86, 352; Yver, *Egalité entre héritiers*; Le Roy Ladurie, "Family and Inheritance"; Quantin, "Recherches sur le tiers-état," p. 42.

94. On Abbot Geoffroy's character, the *Chronique* is informative: late in life Geoffroy was constantly at odds with his monks, evidently feeling them to be unworthy of his redone church. He tried to bring in "foreigners," a policy that led to a formal protest. He arranged for his burial to take place at the foot of Archbishop Hugues of Sens who had carried through the construction of the great cathedral, an indication of his own view of himself as a great builder. It would probably not be too much to say that he became obsessed with the church as he aged. On these points, see *Chronique*, pp. 477, 554; *Livre des reliques*, pp. 84–86.

95. Berman, *Law and Revolution*, p. 320; Cipolla, *Before the Industrial Revolution*, p. 146.

96. Bloch, "Liberté et servitude," p. 299.

97. *Livre des reliques*, pp. 82–87.

98. On Valuisant, AD: Yonne H 684, 710. On Sainte-Colombe, BM: Sens MS 44, p. 368: "fuerint furati [in 1289] calices thesauri ecclesie beate columbe et per miracula domini . . . inventi fuerunt."

99. Hilton, *English Peasantry*, pp. 63, 70; *Decline of Serfdom*, p. 25; *Bond Men Made Free*; Raban, *Mortmain Legislation*, p. 6; Razi, "Struggles," pp. 151–67.

100. "Inter nos et dictos homines et feminas bonis mediantibus et domini regis interveniente consensu hujusmodi composicio intervenit."

101. Geremek, *Les Marginaux*; Cohen, "Patterns of Crime," pp. 307–27.

CHAPTER 4
Arranging to Pay

1. *Histoire de la France rurale*, 1:531–32; Hilton, *Bond Men Made Free*, p. 82.

2. Ryerson, "Changes in Testamentary Practices," p. 266.

3. Kaeuper, *Bankers to the Crown*, pp. 27–46.

4. Still the best overall introduction to the subject of credit remains De Roover, *Money, Banking and Credit*.

5. *Rdp*, nos. 561 (dated 1256), 659 (dated 1270); AD: Yonne, G 2311 MS dated 1258; AD: Yonne, H 51 MS 7 (dated 1257).

6. Below, text to nn.9, 17.

7. *Rdp*, no. 304, dated 1224, "ecclesie prenotate et quitarunt granchiam suam . . . cum fossatis et porprisia granchie . . . post decessum . . . quiete in perpetuum possidendam."

8. See, for example, of those listed in the last paragraph the grant to Chablis (1258), which lists thirty-nine representatives of the community, but the total size of the community is not given; AD: Yonne, G 2311. Also *Rdp*, nos. 561, 659.

9. The record (AD: Yonne, H 51 MS 7) explicitly notices twenty-four family groups by listing a series of names and the kin relationship: e.g., "Simon gener Alberici, Albericus Pinart, Petrus filius eius." Clustering of surnames, without explicit mention of family relationships, occurs twenty-eight times. I may have missed some examples where the scribe slipped and used a French surname that I did not recognize as equivalent to a Latin form in this usually Latinizing record. Two examples that I did spot will illustrate the problem: H. Ferdasne is listed in proximity to B. Asinarius (French *fer d'asne* = Latin *asinarius*); Hodeardis La Clateliere is listed in proximity to Felisius Claviger (French [fem.] *clatelière* = Latin [masc.] *claviger*). One hundred three people are included in these various groups, leaving 263 people, many of whom might have been fairly closely related. The "four pounds or so" estimate reflects the generous estimate that as many as one hundred family groups may be hidden here, bringing the total number of such groups to one hundred fifty or so having to raise 500 l. p. per year. Expressed in the normal money of payment (*tournois*) of 625 l. per year, we may be talking about 4 l. t. per family, per year for twelve years.

10. AD: Yonne, G 940, 941 (accounts for 1295, 1317).

11. Cf. Jones, "Harvest Customs" (both articles).

12. *HF*, 21:274 (royal accounts for the 1240s).

13. Orchards: AD: Yonne, G 1488, various MSS in a packet marked "Chapitre de Sens . . . Paroisse St. Pregts . . . (1236)"; cf. the Sénonais village with the delightful name, Cerisiers (Cherrytrees). Willow thickets and brakes: AD: Yonne, H 320, internal packet, "Sens, Abbaye de Saint Remy, 1235 Villemanoche," MS marked on paper flyleaf "1235"; *Livre des revenus*, pp. 207–8. Groves (probably alder groves, cf. *Dictionnaire topographique: Yonne*, pp. iii–iv): AD: Yonne, H 181, three pages from end; *Livre des revenus*, pp. 172, 189, 195, 202, 215. Small forests: above, n.10.

14. A tanning mill apparently flourished, "Les Botoarii"; *Livre des revenus*, index (cf. Godefroy [rev.], *Lexique*, s.v. "bouton"). Willows provided tannin as well as withes for baskets and material for folk cures (cf. Bowness, *Romany Magic*, p. 54). In general, see Birrell, "Peasant Craftsmen in the Medieval Forest," p. 92.

15. *Histoire de la France rurale*, 1:518–21. The best discussion is Kosminsky, *Studies*, pp. 230–40, and similar English explorations, as Hilton, *Decline of Serfdom*, pp. 12–13, 32, 37 n.3; Hilton, *Bond Men Made Free*, p. 37; Titow, *English Rural Society*, p. 80; Britton, *Community of the Vill*, pp. 135–37, 157–63; Dyer, *Lords and Peasants*, pp. 64, 72, 90, 110; Birrell, "Peasant Craftsmen," pp. 105–6.

16. Below, n.80.

17. AD: Yonne, G 2311, "promiserunt solvere pro quolibet termino in quo in solutione defecerint centum libras turonenses interesse."

18. AD: Yonne, H 51 MS 7, "ad penam viginti solidorum parisiensium pro qualibet die qua cessatum fuerit de integra solucione facienda post terminos supradictos ad quam penam solvendam se obligaverunt erga nos homines supradicti."

19. BM: Auxerre, MS 217, pp. 367–70 (examples of the abbey of Sainte-Colombe's penalty clauses).

20. *Histoire de la France rurale*, 1:529. Cf. Hilton, *Bond Men Made Free*, p. 84.

21. AN: J 261 no. 13: References to "Gaudins pleges" for an amount totalling in excess of 130 s. p. "Le prestre de saint Hylaire" stood for 13 s.; and a "Mestre Nicholas de Chastiau Landon" stood for 40 s. Cf. also, "Li taillierres de Torigni pleges per sire Vilain Bertranz de Vilois iiii s. par" and "Li tiliers de Torigni pleges." The total amounts being assured exceeded 300 s. p.

22. AD: Yonne, F 441, "Copies de Coutume et Etablissements de rentes à la ville de Sens."

23. Turlan, *Commune . . . de Sens*, p. 27; Larcher de Lavernade, *Histoire de la ville de Sens*, p. 86.

24. Taveau, *Cartulaire sénonais*, p. 63.

25. AN: J 261 no. 13, "Item En devoit. LX. XIX lb. IIII s. enpruntez."

26. On the career of Guillaume, above, chap. 3, nn.46–52; On the general points, Sivéry, *Economie du royaume de France*, pp. 223, 225–26, 257–60.

27. AD: Yonne, H 51 MS 7, "Et fiet soluc[i]o nobis vel mandato nostro Parisius in domo Hospitalis."

28. Prütz, "Finanziellen Operationen der Hospitaliter," pp. 17–47. Cf. Delisle, *Opérations financières des Templiers*, pp. 24–40.

29. AD: Yonne, G 2311, MS of 1258, "pro se et universis et singulis burgensibus, hominibus et habitatoribus predicte ville"; "pagaturos et integraliter soluturos [dominis] . . . apud Pruvinium."

30. Possibly noticed in *Rdp*, no. 659, "se plegios obligaverunt."

31. In general on credit and manumission: Duby, "Medieval Agriculture," p. 208; Kosminsky, *Studies*, p. 252.

32. For example, *Rdp*, no. 573 (year 1247, vidimus of 1257), "verumtamen ubicumque ibunt, vel manebunt, tenebuntur reddere, ut dictum est, dictos duodecim denarios tur., pro dicta libertate."

33. Cf. Valous, *Temporel*, p. 103, for the Burgundian evidence.

34. *Rdp*, no. 403 (year 1232), "quilibet eorum . . . persolvat annuatim mihi decem solidos censualis monete . . . et quatuor bichetos annone."

35. "Si, vero, ad dictum terminum, dictos duodecim denarios non redderent, quilibet ipsorum deficiens in solucione, ut dictum est, facienda, teneretur reddere quinque solidos turon. pro emenda."

36. AD: Yonne, G 1378; E 622 (various copies), "remiserunt et quitaverunt in recompensationem predictorum spontanei non coacti . . . ducenta arpenta nemorum in usariis suis cum duobus arpentis pro viis et plateis eisdem ducentis arpentis contiguis juncta nemoribus dictorum decani et capituli de Sociaco." To determine the size of the Sénonais arpent, I have consulted an "Enquête" of 1626, a "Plan" of 1768, and a later "Plan" of 1796 (AD: Yonne, G 1361, 1389). I have collated the information with that assembled by Jones, "Land Measurement," pp. 10–18.

37. *Rdp*, no. 136. See below, nn.65–75, for further discussion.

38. *Rdp*, no. 362, "Unusquisque solvat michi . . . quatuor denarios pro qualibet libra valoris tenure sue. . . . Si quis . . . solvere voluerit centum solidos, jurare propter hoc non cogetur, set quitus erit de conventionibus predictis." No. 391, "de chascun sis deniers de la livre do meuble . . . et deus deniers de la livre de l'éritage, chascun an." For the selection of local authorities, the passage begins, "Et est à savoir que gie, au autres de mes genz, ellirons chacun an treze homes de la comuneté de Saint-Florentin à bone foi, et cile treze elliront l'un d'aus à maieur chascun an. . . ."

39. AD: Yonne, E 576 (*Rdp*, no. 702), "de taille que nous avyons sur eulx à nostre voulente, à hault et bas, en biens meubles et non meubles, en telle manière que cil qui porra paier quinze sols de tornois les nous paiera pour raison de la franchise, et de plus ne les pouvons ne devons enfforcier ly plus pouvres ou ly moins puissans deux sols t. . . . Et voulons que quatre personnes soyent eslys, deulx de par nous ou de par nostre prévost ou chastellain, et deulx de par de nosdiz hommes. . . ."

40. AD: Yonne, H 711 MS of 1271, "a quolibet ipsorum levare poterunt si levare voluerint quinque solidos turonenses de emenda."

41. AD: Yonne, E 550 (*Rdp*, no. 701); the discussion of selection procedures is extremely long and very picky.

42. AD: Yonne, G 1697, MS of 1283, "Quas centum libras nobis solvent predicti homines nostri in hunc modum singulis enim annis eligentur tres viri probi et ydonei . . . ex parte hominum predictorum et tres alii . . . ex parte nostra qui

. . . consideratis viribus et facultatibus hominum . . . porcionem congruam assignabunt."

43. AN: J 261 no. 13; see table 4.1.

44. All references to the list of the defaulters, whose names are in French, are to the roll cited in the preceding note; many of these may be checked against the Latinized forms in the manumission of 1257 (AD: Yonne, H 51 MS 7). It is the manumission that identifies parishes of residence in general, "in burgo nostro Sancti Petri Vivi Senonensis, in parrochia sancti saviniani et apud Malleotum Sancti Petri Vivi." In subsequent notes, the entry will be given first according to the French roll, then from the Latin manumission, though I will try to avoid unnecessary repetition. For the people mentioned thus far in the text: Pierres Malebeste v s./Petrus Malebeste; Jehannez Coifete xii d./Johannes Coiffete.

45. Thiebaut Fillon xii d./Theobaldus Fillon.

46. Gilez langue dame xii d./Gilo Longa Domina.

47. Li fillastres a la fame feu Morise xii d./Stephanus filius defuncti Mauricii. On Jean Letardi, below, n.55.

48. Jordan, "Communal Administration," pp. 293–95. By the Treaty of Paris the English king ratified the loss of Normandy to the French in the early thirteenth century. The English king agreed to this for an indemnity in excess of 100,000 French pounds, which the French raised by an impost on communes like Sens.

49. "Default de mise dou don lou roi faite en lan de grace M CC LIX Estienne Dalemant Garde de la merie de Senz."

50. Jehannez Coifete xii d.; Thiebauz Fillons xii d.; Gilez Longue Dame xii d.; La fillatres a la fame feu Morise xii d.

51. Felis Cartauz xii d./Felisius Cartale.

52. La fame feu Morise xii d.

53. This example provides an opportunity to reveal some of the difficulties that confront the researcher who tries to explore matters like this through a collation of manumission lists, obituary books, and fragmentary accounts in the absence of the rather more straightforward data available from, say, English manor court rolls. In fact, the name Raoulet Le Lavandier of the parish of Saint-Savinian of Sens does not appear on the manumission as a single individual. There we find the entry, "children of Lavandier" (*pueri Lavendarii*). However, launderer or in modern French Le Lavandier, although perhaps an occupation practiced in the family, was in the process of becoming a surname. In the obituary book known as the *Book of Revenues* (pp. 174, 176) one discovers that a woman called La Lavandière held property of Saint-Pierre that rented for 16 d. p. She does not seem to have been a dependent of the abbey. Also holding with her were the "children of the late Adam, a janitor" (*liberi defuncti, Ade, janitoris*); janitor referred to a menial occupation but not necessarily to a janitor in the modern sense. The children paid 8 d.t. rent on this property which, as far as I can tell, seems to have been located at a spot geographically appropriate for the holding that the children of Le Lavandier possessed according to the arrangement of names on the manumission, but this is not a certainty. What would settle the issue would be to find out that Adam's last name was in fact Le Lavandier. A different manuscript of the *Book of Revenues* (variant readings at p. 174 n. 1) informs us that on the death of La Lavandière, the total

property was held by the children: Gilles (Guiot) Le Lavandier, Jean d'Ervy, Raoulet Le Lavandier, Jacquète La Lavandière and Eudes (Odim) Le Charretier. Three seem to have kept the occupational surname of their mother, although whether they actually followed the trade of the launderer may be doubted. One assumed a geographical surname; and the last took a different occupational surname. The manuscript also informs us that Jacquète's father was Adam Le Lavandier. These children were freed by the manumission in 1257 (their individual names not being given); one of them shows up as a defaulter on the *mise* of 1259 for the minimum levy: Raoulez li Lavandiers xii d.

54. 1258: Estienne Turmiaus por sa fame xii d.; 1259: Estienne Trumiaus por sa fame xii d. Manumission: Stephanus Trumel.

55. 1258: Jehanz Lietarz por sa fame v s.; 1259: Jehans Lietarz ii s. et di. Manumission: Johannes Letardi.

56. 1258: Jehan Turmiau por sa fame iii s.; 1259: Jehanz Trumiaus por sa fame xviii d. Manumission: Johannes Trumiaus.

57. Giry, *Documents*, p. 101, no. 36.

58. AD: Yonne, H 376, especially fols. 10 v. – 38 v.

59. *Chronique*, p. 528, "contra usurarios sententias excommunicationum ostiatim viriliter per dioecesim et civitatem provulgabat. . . . Iste . . . sustentator pauperum et amator."

60. Ibid., "et, ut dicunt quidam, veneno extinguetur." *Recueil des statuts*, p. 36; Bouvier, *Histoire de l'Eglise . . . de Sens*, pp. 240–41.

61. Jordan, *Louis IX*, pp. 84–86, 116, 154–57; Jordan, "An Aspect of Credit," pp. 141–52. Cf. also on consumer credit, *Histoire de la France rurale*, 1:524–26.

62. Chartraire, "Prisons de l'Officialité," pp. 100, 103, 105–6, 116–17, 122; Fournier, *Officialités*, p. 61; Fourrey, *Sens*, pp. 100–101.

63. The Jews were among the wealthiest members of the community at the turn of the twelfth to the thirteenth century; Porée, *Histoire des rues*, pp. 289–302, summarizes some of the material in a discussion of the streets inhabited by the medieval Jews. A few of his more general remarks on the status of the Jews are suspect. The community was small but tenacious toward the end of the thirteenth century, inhabiting a *ruella judearie*, a *platea de judearia*, which made a kind of definite section of the city (*tres camere . . . que faciunt conum judearie*). They still possessed a grange or farm (*granchia judearie*). But the community was dissolved in 1306 with the expulsions; and the cemetery was sold in 1308. AD: Yonne, H 306 (Censier Saint-Remy, ca. 1300), fols. 30 v., 31, 32; Larcher de Lavernade, *Histoire de la ville de Sens*, p. 94.

64. Some records have been discovered in the bindings of books. The matter is discussed in Jordan, "Jewish-Christian Relations," p. 48. Most of the investigations into Jewish activities per se took place in 1247 and 1248, but there is evidence that this aspect of the inquiry persisted at least until 1260 in some regions; brief mentions only have survived of Sénonais investigations in 1255 and 1257. See *HF*, vol. 24, "Préface," pp. 5, 6, 9.

65. *Rdp*, no. 136. For a discussion of how this fits in with the policies of the manumitting lord, see Sassier, *Recherches*, p. 121.

66. The act is referred to 1236 in *Rdp*, no. 1009, but it appears that Lebeuf,

Mémoires, vol. 2, "Recueil de monumens," p. 280, publishes the grant under the year 1234. I have not been able to verify the citation in *Rdp*. Nevertheless, the liabilities under which the other inhabitants suffered do not seem to have been as debasing as those from which the inhabitants were delivered in 1214.

67. *Rdp*, no. 136, "Predicti, vero, homines ville predicte tradent famulo, vel ministro terre, quintam-decimam partem vindemie."

68. "Sane qui plantare vineam voluerit ab anno incarnationis Domini M° CC° XX°, pro quolibet arpento dabit quinque solidos et unum sextarium vini servientibus." The location in woodlands is inferred from the long discussion earlier in the record on rights in woodlands adjacent to Sacy: "Cultores . . . colligent de omni nemore," "boscum necessarium," "de bosco mortuo," "usuarium suum in meo nemore sicco," "boscos, vero, meos," "ad boscum," etc. The location is confirmed by the text quoted at n.71.

69. See, e.g., below, text to n.81.

70. Quantin, *Cartulaire général*, 2:62, 64; *Rdp*, no. 157.

71. *Rdp*, no. 240, "in nemore nobilis viri Ascelini de Merriaco, quod est situm in finagio de Saciaco . . . homines de Saciaco partem illius nemoris extirpaverant et ad culturam redegerant . . . quod, per factum ipsorum, in extirpata ab eis parte predicti nemoris, suum usuagium amisissent."

72. Ibid., "ipsos traxerunt in causam coram judicibus auctoritate apostolica delegatis, petentes sibi ab eisdem hominibus emendari."

73. Ibid., "Tandem, vero post multos labores parcium et expensas."

74. Ibid., "compromissione in nos facta, nobis [=episcopo] mediantibus, de communi assensu parcium inter ipsos compositum est in hunc modum: Dicti abbas et conventus omne dampnum et injuriam que in extirpatione predicta illata sibi fuerant, dictis hominibus penitus remiserunt, concedentes ut iidem homines quicquid in quocunque parte dicti nemoris, usque ad tempus hujus compositionis extirpaverant, ab omni contradictione ipsorum et calumpnia pacifice de cetero possiderent, et si citra locum qui dicitur Vallis-Putei, a parte Saciaci, aliquid de empcione ipsorum adhuc esset extirpandum, illud possent libere extirpare. Sed ultra predictum locum, scilicet Vallem-Putei, nichil de cetero poterunt extirpare."

75. Ibid.: note the reference to those who may have made an agreement with the monks otherwise than in the compromise under discussion, "Verum, si ab illis qui non sunt in hac compositione vel alias cum dictis abbate et conventu non composuerint."

76. Doinel, *Cartulaire de . . . Voisins*, pp. 7, 41–43.

77. *Olim*, 1:26 xiv.

78. Also Lebeuf, *Mémoires*, vol. 2, "Recueil de monumens," pp. 41, 46 nos. 88, 99.

79. *Rdp*, no. 573.

80. AD: Yonne, H 225, internal packet entitled "Titres de droits de cens sur biens (1262)," MS marked on the reverse with a faint J. The parties to the lease were Adam dictus Piaz and his wife and the freedmen (cf. AD: Yonne, H 51 MS 7) Johannes dictus Pyaz, Jacobus dictus Heremita, Stephanus and Petrus dicti de Monasterio, and their wives. The lease reads, with regard to rents, "dicebant et se

tenebant integre pro pagatis quodlibet arpentum pro quadraginta solidis turonensibus annui redditus reddendis . . . obligantes quantum ad hoc dictis religiosis se et heredes suos et dictam vineam et possessiones que sequntur. . . ."

81. *Rdp*, no. 649 (with minor errors of transcription corrected here): "tradiderant quandam peciam terre continentem novem arpenta . . . pro vineis in dicta terra plantandis seu domibus edificandis . . . scilicet cuilibet predictorum hominum unum arpentum et octavam partem unius arpenti excepto Odone Reborrerio cui tradiderunt modo predicto duo arpenta dicte terre et duas partes duorum arpentorum pro quindecim solidis parisiensibus pro unoquoque arpento. . . . Et si per duos annos continuos defuerint in solutione . . . dicti religiosi . . . dictam vineam vel domum . . . saisire poterunt." Cf. Decret. Greg. IX, Lib. III, Tit. XVIII, cap. IV.

82. On the property of Adam; *Livre des revenus*, pp. 129, 163–64, 196, 205, 219, 227. On the property of Petrus Geste (Jeste, Geite, Geîte), ibid., pp. 188, 190, 210, 214.

83. On the manumission Gilles Boons appears in the Latin form Gilo Boon. The property transactions are noticed in ibid., pp. 170, 173, where his name regularly appears as a diminutive: Guyotus Bouns, Guillotus Boons. The entries for tenants on p. 170 closes with the word *Vacat* in a later hand, probably the hand of the scribe who recorded the Pierre Geîte entries, referred to earlier (hence, my tentative suggestion for dating).

84. AD: Yonne, H 181, p. 9, "Laurencius de Ruella vi s. pro uno quarterio terre sedenti ad bordellum de Maleyo."

85. Lhuillier, "Inventaire des titres," p. 352. Manumission: Laurencius de Ruella and Petrus filius Laurencii de Ruella. For the holdings of Notre-Dame-du-Lys, see AD: Seine-et-Marne, H 576, "Inventaire des titres et papiers de la terre et seigneurie de Mallay," pp. 95–97 (cf. also pp. 1–76, 98–102).

86. Cartage: payments to Lambert Coiffete (manumission: Lambertus Coiffete) and Pierre de Ruelle of 4 l. 12 d. t. and 5 l. 8 s.; *HF*, 22:672–736 (accounts of royal armies' march south over the Yonne, during the crossing of which a horse was lost in the river, "mort à Yone"; the entry for Lambert and Pierre is at p. 731). On the obit: *Livre des revenus*, p. 168, "Obiit Petrus de Rueil pro quo habet conventus x s. t. super prata de Beissiaco." In a different manuscript of this obituary, the place name appears as Bessiacum; in a third version, Baissiacum. See *Livre des revenus*, p. 168 n.2; and BM: Auxerre, MS 214 (ancien 181), fol. 7 r.

87. Manumission: Clara uxor Hylarii Gaignart.

88. The scribe records the anniversary in the following manner: "Obiit Clara, uxor Hylarii Guignart, pro qua habet conventus, super vineam de Chaliel, ii s. t." The succession of tenants is my own reconstruction based on information in the *Livre des revenus* at pp. 194, 204 (the manuscript has a defect at Gilles's last name, but a Gilles Gaignart is documented in other records).

89. Nicholas, "Patterns of Social Mobility," p. 77.

90. Postan's chapter ("The Villagers: Serfdom and Freedom") in *Medieval Economy and Society*, pp. 143–55, is perhaps the most maddening contrary view to the argument presented here. While acknowledging the resentments toward

serfdom, he downplays the priority of freedom (or free status) as an ideal. This conclusion is based on the fact that a serf "could always improve his economic condition by buying from his lord a charter of manumission" (p. 143). Since the vast proportion of the peasantry did not go that route in thirteenth-century England and since some evidence survives of voluntary debasement of status, "we are driven to the conclusion that freedom was not always estimated more highly than, or even as highly as, material possessions" (p. 144). What is completely left out of the analysis is the resistance of the lords to granting manumission or, equally likely, their demands of extremely high purchase prices. It is not enough to answer this last objection, as Postan answered it, namely, by concluding that since some serfs did buy manumissions, most of them could have paid for them if they really cherished freedom above all other values: "high as the price of manumission sometimes was, it was seldom so high as to be beyond the means of more substantial villagers, and not higher than the prices they sometimes paid for additional land" (p. 143).

CHAPTER 5
Residual Problems

1. Quantin's headnotes to the document (*Rdp*, no. 550) completely misrepresent its contents.

2. "Gaufridus, filius defuncti Hayeri de Evriaco, quem, ut dicebat idem Gaufridus, capitulum Senon. manumiserat ad hoc ut posset habere tonsuram et ordinem clericalem . . . tali condicione quod si contingeret ipsam tonsuram clericalem dimittere, ipso facto in pristinam conditionem et ad hominium [*sic*] dicti capituli revertetur; promittens, dictus Gaufridus, per fidem suam in manu nostra prestitam, quod dictam conditionem servabit, nec contra predicta veniet in futurum." This record was filed in what is now bundle G 729 of the archives of the Yonne along with the recognition on status descent referred to in the text and discussed below, nn. 21–24.

3. *Rdp*, no. 641, "Johannes . . . a dicto capitulo manumissus dixit et asseruit coram nobis, quod capitulum Senon., vel aliquam personam dicti capituli seu etiam homines ipsorum non citabit vel vexabit, nec in aliquo molestabit de cetero nisi coram ordinariis suis; omnia bona sua, ubicunque sint et poterunt inveniri, quantum ad hoc specialiter obligando. Voluit eciam et concessit, dictus Johannes, quod si ipsum contigerit uxorem ducere, vel tonsuram dimittere clericalem, quod ad priorem statum . . . penitus revertatur."

4. AD: Yonne, G 1378 (E 622), "et ex nunc licentiati tonsuram clericalem tamen de manu prefati possint accipere et deferre."

5. From within the Ermite family (Latin Heremita), the Rousel (Rosselli) family, and the de Buisson (de Dumo) family which were freed in the mid-century (AD: Yonne, H 51 MS 7: Jacobus Heremita, Jacobus Roselli, Galterus de Dumo), the following instances are possible examples, although the documentation is thin:

(1) *Magister* Jean Ermite, *clericus*, attests the purchase of a fief by Guillaume Dalle-mant in 1270; *Rdp*, no. 664. (2) Guillaume Ermite, *presbyter canonicus* of the cathe-dral of Sens, had his obit celebrated on 10 Kalends January; BM: Sens, MS 45. (3) *Magister* Gérard Rousel, *clericus*, is described as a property holder in the manumission of the serfs of Saint-Julien-du-Sault; *Rdp*, no. 659. (4) *Magister* Geoffroy de Buisson is listed under crown debtors in Sens in 1308; *Comptes royaux*, vol. 2, no. 15424.

6. *Rdp*, no. 304, "ut ipsi liberi sint ab omni tallia et corveia et omni servitute corporali . . . et nos ipsos et heredes eorum quos ex propriis genuerint . . . recepimus sub dictis libertatibus."

7. *Rdp*, no. 695, "predictum Stephanum et ejus heredes manumiserant, liberaverant et quitaverant ab omni onere, servicio et servitute."

8. *Rdp*, no. 691, "pensata utilitate ecclesiae nostrae remisimus manum mor-tuam. . . . volumus pro nobis successoribusque nostris, predictis hominibus et feminabus in hoc expresse consentientibus, quod predictae manus-mortuae re-missio et ea que in predictis litteris [of manumission] continentur non possunt pre-dicto capitulo in villis et rebus suis prejudicium grave innotare . . . ; et quod homines nostri dictarum villarum hactenus acquisierint vel acquirent in futurum, vel accipient in maritagium res aliquas in villis seu locis ubi habet manum-mortuam dictum capitulum, et decedent sine herede de proprio corpore derelicto: quod res sic acquisitas existentes in manu-mortua dicti capituli mobiles et immo-biles, in omnibusque et singulis casibus uti de consuetudine habet locum manus-mortua, dictum capitulum acciperet et suas faceret absque reclamatione ali-quorum praedictorum hominum et feminarum, vel heredum suorum." See also Nicholas, "Patterns of Social Mobility," p. 77.

9. See the discussion accompanying *Rdp*, no. 719.

10. AD: Yonne, H 265, MSS in packet marked "1276 La Veille de la Pente-coste." For other references, above, chap. 2, n.24.

11. Claire is referred to as *uxor* not *relicta* or *vidua* of her husband in AD: Yonne, H 51 MS 7. There are twenty-five similar examples.

12. It could not have arisen from marriages between those who were freed by Saint-Pierre and others, not freed, on its manors (above, chap. 3, nn.59–60) be-cause the wives of manorialized dependents lived on the manors with their hus-bands and were not covered by the manumission.

13. "Stephanus Pes Latoris pro uxore sua"; "Johannes gener Stephani Claudi pro uxore sua"; "Rogerus de Sancto Praiecto pro uxore sua"; "Garinus Morel pro uxore sua"; "Bernardus de Capella pro uxore sua."

14. Above, chap. 4, nn.54–56.

15. *Rdp*, no. 285, "Si, vero, contigeret homines abbatis feminabus dicti Dro-conis, vel contra homines ipsius Droconis feminabus abbatis matrimonialiter copulari, liberi qui ex tali copula fuerint procreati, cum omnibus bonis eorum generaliter per medium inter eosdem dominos dividentur."

16. *Rdp*, no. 412, "quod ipsa Florentia et medietas omnium liberorum qui ex ea nati sunt et nascituri sunt . . . liberi et abboniati. . . . quinque solidos pruvin. nomine abboniationis solvere tenebuntur . . . et qui . . . defecerit in solutione

abboniationis predicte, defectum illum per alios quinque solidos tenebitur emendare."

17. AD: Yonne, H 287. Quantin's inventory calls the man "Robert, sergent de Pont-sur-Vanne" as if sergeant were an occupation. The manuscript actually reads, "Robertus dictus Serviens." In another document dealing with this family (*Rdp*, no. 592), Quantin reads *dit Sergent* as *dit Sagur*.

18. *Olim*, 1:117, "Abbas et conventus predicti nichil probant, et nichil habeant." See also AD: Yonne, G 54bis MS 41.

19. Bernardus de Capella purchased his wife's freedom; and this information is enrolled on the manumission in a cluster of names including Maria uxor Isamberti. The de Capella neighbor of this Maria is identified in other sources as a *valletus*; AD: Yonne, H 218, MSS entitled "1278 Censives et Coutumes de Beaumont" and "de costumis apud pontes pro Gaufrido abbate."

20. *Rdp*, no. 596, "erat homo dicti domini Senon. pro toto . . . et erat femina domini regis pro medietate, ex parte patris sui quondam burgensis dicti domini regis, et femina dicti domini Senon. pro alia medietate, ex parte matris burgensis ejusdem domini Senon. . . . quinque solidorum paris. . . . annis singulis, solvere teneantur, tali modo, quod altero dictorum Johannis et Izabellae, viam universae carnis ingresso, superstes ad duos solidos et dimidium paris. solummodo teneatur."

21. *Rdp*, nos. 550, 597, "recesserat et sub alio dominio seu justicie se transtulerat, scilicet sub dominio regis, apud Villam-Novam, quod facere non poterat nec debebat, ut dicebat, cum ipse esset homo ipsorum decani et capituli pro medietate ex parte matris."

22. "fuisset diutius altercatum"; "nec poterit ultra hoc . . . aliquid exigere, petere, vel etiam extorquere."

23. "malo ductus consilio"; "de bonorum consilio . . . reversus erat, et eisdem emendaverat."

24. Above, n.2.

25. *Rdp*, no. 717.

26. AD: Yonne G 1378 (E 622), "Et quod similiter venerabilis vir Albericus Cornuti thesaurarius ecclesie senonensis ad preces et requisitionem dictorum decani et capituli et dictorum hominum suorum de dicto loco ipsos homines suos a jugo servitutis taillie et manusmortue manumisit et quitavit eorumque liberos procreatos et omnem eorum posteritatem imposterum procreandam." (*Rdp*, no. 719, contains a slightly different transcription.)

27. Cf. Duby, "Diffusion of Cultural Patterns," pp. 6–7.

28. AD: Yonne, G 1697, "omnes homines jure naturali inspecto gaudere debent privilegio libertatis ac inter ceteros fidei christiani ministros ecclesia utpote mater omnium fidelium privilegium libertatis non solum tenetur concedere sed eciam ab aliis Christi fidelibus concessum protegere et tueri justa sacrorum canonum instituta ac legum secularium legitimas sanctiones."

29. Lebeuf, *Mémoires*, vol. 2, "Recueil de monumens," p. 66, no. 145.

30. E.g., Hilton, *Decline of Serfdom*, pp. 24–25.

31. The phrase "mystique about freedom" is Nicholas's, "Patterns of Social Mobility," p. 75.

32. Felisius and Felisia, 20:366. Johannes and Johanna, 41:366; Stephanus, 35:366; Petrus and Petronilla, 22:366.

33. Odo, 19:366; Gilo and Gila, 13:366; Jacobus (including variants, Jaqernus, Jaqerus, Jaquinus), 13:366; Theobaldus, 13:366; Thomas, 10:366.

34. AN: J 261 no. 13.

35. AD: Yonne, G 144 MS 2, "Felisius presbyter, capellanus capelle regis Senonensis."

36. Cf. Lhuillier's "Inventaire des titres," pp. 348, 351; but when I have been able to verify Lhuillier's rather poorly referenced charters against the originals, they frequently pertain to *freed* people. See, e.g., above, chap. 4, n.85.

37. *Rdp*, nos. 628, 668, 714, list no names. The manuscripts show that the first has about 200, the second 50, and the third about 150 (AD: Yonne, G 1340, H 711, G 1697).

38. Inferred from the manumission of Soucy, involving well over 300 people and partly intended to bring spouses of out-marriages into freedom (above, n.26). Again, Quantin's published edition of the record suppresses 330 names. The manuscript may be consulted in AD: Yonne G 1378 (E 622).

39. BM: Sens, MS 45; *Kalendarium*, pp. 128–29, 138, 145. Cf. Carrez, "Noms de personne féminins," p. 115.

40. BM: Sens, MS 24, "Ceremoniale Antiquum S. Petri Vivi," p. 113 (dated variously 12th/13th century; cf. the unpublished library inventory); *Livre des reliques*, pp. 4–5, 9, 10, 29, 40, 58, 61, 73–74, 76; *Kalendarium*, pp. 125, 140, 143, 150; and the citations above, n.39.

41. "La verve gauloise": Quantin in *Rdp*, p. xxviii. On the supposed meaning of *félis* in popular speech, see Moiset, "Essai sur l'origine des noms . . . particulièrement dans la région de l'Yonne," pp. 48–49.

42. Converted Jews in the thirteenth century became godchildren of the king, and so they were baptized under his saint's name; Grayzel, *Church and the Jews*, p. 285 n.1. The information on Pleasant comes from *Black Names in America*, pp. 52, 76, 96.

43. *Livre des revenus*, p. 227.

44. AD: Yonne, H 225 (*recognitio* of 1249); cf. above, chap. 3, nn.41–43.

45. Manumission: Felisia relicta Stephani Borgoing, *Livre des revenus*, index.

46. On the whole the reader must accept this point on faith. A certain F. (Felisius?) Archiepiscopi of *Livre des revenus*, pp. 196, 205, is not probably an exception, for although he may have been related to the widow of Dominic Archevèque and Gilles Archevèque (both manumitted: "Relicta defuncti Domenici Archiepiscopi, Gilo Archiepiscopi"), he had already left a widow according to the early entries in that book. This makes it unlikely that he was born after 1257. A Félisot li Piat (p. 229) was a contemporary of several other "Piats" who were manumitted in 1257 (cf. above, chap. 4, text following n.80). It is unlikely he was born after 1257. I know of no other even possible exceptions, but, of course, I may inadvertently have missed some.

47. AD: Yonne, G 1378 (E 622, p. 5; *Rdp*, no. 719).

48. BM: Sens, MS 45, p. 317: "domorum que fuerunt defuncti Radulfi dicti

quondam villani." A villein in France (but not England), it is usually said, was technically free, but "from the thirteenth century, however, the villeins became merged increasingly with the serfs" (Nicholas, "Patterns of Social Mobility," p. 75).

49. Entries for Villein Dallemant are enrolled on AN: J 261 no. 13; a Felisius Biauvilain was manumitted in 1257 (above, text preceding n. 32).

50. Paustian, "Evolution of Personal Naming Practices," pp. 184–85; *Black Names in America*, pp. 44–61.

51. Tomasson, "Continuity of Icelandic Names," pp. 282–85.

52. Wormsley, "Tradition and Change in Imbonggu Names and Naming Practices," pp. 191–94.

53. Bennett, *Life on the English Manor*, pp. 3–25 (repr. in Tierney, *Middle Ages*, vol. 2, *Readings*, pp. 167–83).

Epilogue

1. Fourquin, *Lordship and Feudalism*, pp. 183–99; and, more generally, Duby, "Medieval Agriculture," pp. 210–15, for the transformations of the fourteenth century. See also, Pollock and Maitland, *History of English Law*, 1: 382–83.

2. Nicholas, "Patterns of Social Mobility," p. 75; Berman, *Law and Revolution*, pp. 331–32.

3. Duby, "Medieval Agriculture," p. 209. The purchases aggravated the debts; Nicholas, "Patterns of Social Mobility," p. 77.

4. Sivéry, *Saint Louis*, pp. 158–224; Strayer, "Economic Conditions," pp. 277–87.

5. Duby, "Medieval Agriculture," p. 209; Nicholas, "Patterns of Social Mobility," pp. 87–90; Fourquin, *Lordship and Feudalism*, pp. 215–26.

6. Fourquin, *Lordship and Feudalism*, pp. 204–12; Mollat and Wolff, *Popular Revolutions*, pp. 310–12; Eberhard and Seibt, *Europa 1400*, pp. 200–220.

7. Sivéry, *Economie du royaume de France*, pp. 117–33; Henneman, *Royal Taxation*, pp. 12–13.

8. Above, chap. 2, text to nn. 58–61.

9. Henneman, *Royal Taxation*, p. 12, "the great landed interests were quick to oppose inflationary royal policies like coinage debasement."

10. Glenisson and Day, *Textes et documents*, no. 59; Cutler, *Law of Treason*, pp. 32–35. See also Tuchman's *Distant Mirror*.

11. Hilton, *Decline of Serfdom*, p. 34; Sivéry, *Structures agraires*, 2: 380, 405–511. See also Razi, *Economy*, pp. 110–13, 146–48; Harvey, *Westminster Abbey*, chap. 9; DeWindt, *Land and People*, chap. 2.

12. Artonne, *Mouvement de 1314*, p. 31; Denisova-Khachaturian, "Sotsial'no-politicheskie aspekty," p. 170; Henneman, *Royal Taxation*, p. 80. Also Nicholas, "Patterns of Social Mobility," pp. 87, 90; Hilton, *Decline of Serfdom*, pp. 24–25.

13. Larcher de Lavernade, *Histoire de la ville de Sens*, p. 95.

14. Pissier, "Abbaye Notre-Dame de Dilo," p. 85; Biraben, *Hommes et la peste*, 1:78, 85, 377.

15. See, e.g., AD: Yonne, F 280, H 169; AD: Indre, A 20.

16. Cailleaux, "Histoire des Célestins de Sens," p. 14; Bouvier, "Histoire de Saint-Pierre-le-Vif," p. 142.

17. BM: Sens, MS 44, p. 374 (1433), "fuit igne cremata domus de sancta Columba apud Regniacum sita. per quendam furem et homicidam cognorantum le beschat."

Bibliography

Manuscript Sources

AD: Aube (Troyes)—9 H 4, 9 H 77, 24 H 25, 24 H 34
AD: Indre (Châteauroux)—A 20, H 181
AD: Nièvre (Nevers)—32 H 7, II 1
AD: Seine-et-Marne (Melun)—H 576
AD: Vienne (Poitiers)—1 H 5 liasse 3, 1 H 13 liasse 18
AD: Yonne (Auxerre)

    E—357, 550, 558, 576, 615, 622, 636

    E supplément—DD 1

    F—5, 30, 92, 217–18, 280, 412, 441, 474

    G—1, 41, 54bis, 105–6, 119, 135, 144, 533, 726, 729, 940–41, 1124, 1204–5, 1247, 1282, 1310, 1314–15, 1328, 1330, 1340, 1351, 1358–64, 1378, 1389–90, 1421, 1475–76, 1478–79, 1485, 1488, 1511, 1697, 2311

    H—5, 12, 36 à 41, 97, 105, 108, 111, 144, 167, 169–70, 176, 178, 181, 198–200, 204–5, 210–15, 218, 221, 225, 227, 234, 243, 246, 253, 265, 284–85, 287, 297, 301, 303, 306, 313, 320, 376, 403, 408, 415, 418, 429–30, 475, 534, 578, 666, 674, 684, 710–11, 716, 787–88, 790, 946, 1284, 1493

    H supplément—3760–61, 3764, 3771

AN (Paris): J 261 no. 13

BM: Auxerre—MSS 213, 214, 217, 218 (anciens 180, 181, 184, 185)
BM: Sens—MSS 10, 23, 24, 44, 45

Printed Sources

The place of publication for all books, unless otherwise indicated, is Paris.

Bautier, R.-H., and M. Gilles, eds. *Chronique de Saint-Pierre-le-Vif de Sens, dite de Clarius.* 1979.

Beugnot, A., ed. *Les Olim ou Registres des ârrets rendus par la cour du roi.* 1839.

Bouquet, M., et al., eds. *Recueil des historiens des Gaules et de la France.* 24 vols. 1738–1904.

Chartraire, E., ed. *Cartulaire du Chapitre de Sens.* Sens, 1904.

Chronique de l'abbaye de Saint-Pierre-le-Vif de Sens rédigée vers la fin du XIIIe siècle par Geoffroy de Courlon. Edited by G. Julliot. Sens, 1876.

Comptes royaux. 3 vols. Edited by R. Fawtier. 1953–56.

Doinel, J., ed. *Cartulaire de Notre-Dame de Voisins.* Orleans, 1887.

Estienne, C. *La Guide des chemins de France de 1553.* 2 vols. Edited by J. Bonnerot. 1936.

Gallia christiana in provincias ecclesiasticas distributa. 16 vols. 1715–1865.

GC. See *Gallia christiana.*

Giry, A., ed. *Documents sur les relations de la royauté avec les villes en France de 1180 à 1314.* 1885.

Glenisson, J., and J. Day, comps. *Textes et documents d'histoire du moyen âge.* Vol. 2, *Les Structures agraires et la vie rurale.* 1977.

HF. See Bouquet et al.

Julliot, G., ed. *Cartulaire sénonais de Balthasar Taveau.* Sens, 1884.

———. *Inscriptions et monuments du Musée Gallo-Romain de Sens.* Sens, 1898.

———. "Inventaire des saintes reliques et Thrésor de l'abbaye de Saint-Pierre-le-Vif du May 1660." SASens *Bulletin* 11 (1887): 81–105.

Kalendarium. In *Geoffroy de Courlon: Livre des reliques de l'abbaye de Saint-Pierre-le-Vif de Sens.* Edited by G. Julliot and M. Prou. Sens, 1887.

Lalore, C. "Documents pour servir à la généalogie des anciens seigneurs de Traînel." SAAube *Mémoires* 24 (1870): 177–273.

Lebeuf. *Mémoires concernant l'histoire ecclésiastique et civile d'Auxerre.* 2 vols. 1743.

Livre des reliques. See *Kalendarium,* pp. 1–123.

Livre des revenus. See *Kalendarium*, pp. 153–246.

Longnon, A., comp. *Pouillés de la Province de Sens.* 1904.

Molinier, A. *Obituaires de la province de Sens.* 4 vols. in 5 parts. 1902–23.

Olim. See Beugnot.

Quantin, M., ed. *Cartulaire général de l'Yonne.* 2 vols. Auxerre, 1854–60.

———. *Recueil de pièces pour faire suite au Cartulaire général de l'Yonne.* Auxerre and Paris, 1873.

Quesvers, P., and H. Stein, comps. *Inscriptions de l'ancien diocèse de Sens.* 4 vols. 1897–1904.

Rdp. See Quantin, *Recueil.*

Registres du Trésor des chartes. Vol. 1, *Règne de Philippe le Bel.* Edited by R. Fawtier. 1958.

Secondary Sources

The place of publication for all books, unless otherwise indicated, is Paris.

Amé, E. *Les Carrelages émaillés du moyen-âge et de la Renaissance.* 1859.

Arbois de Jubainville, M. d'. *Histoire des ducs et comtes de Champagne.* 6 vols. in 7 parts. 1865.

Artonne, A. *Le Mouvement de 1314 et les chartes provinciales de 1315.* 1912.

Aufauvre, A. *Histoire de Nogent-sur-Seine.* Troyes, 1859.

Baldwin, J. "L'Entourage de Philippe Auguste et la famille royale." In *La France de Philippe Auguste—Le Temps des Mutations.* Colloques internationaux CNRS, no. 602 (1982): 59–75.

Bautier, R.-H. "Guillaume de Mussy, bailli, enquêteur royal, pannetier de France sous Philippe le Bel." *Bibliothèque de l'Ecole de Chartes* 105 (1944): 64–98.

Beckett, J. "The Peasant in England: A Case of Terminological Confusion." *Agricultural History Review* 32 (1984): 113–23.

Benn, S. "The Uses of Sovereignty." In *Political Philosophy*, edited by A. Quinton. Oxford, 1967.

Benton, J. "Philip the Fair and the Jours of Troyes." *Studies in Medieval and Renaissance History* 6 (1969): 279–344.

Berman, H. *Law and Revolution: The Formation of the Western Legal Tradition.* Cambridge, Mass., and London, 1983.

Bernard, G. *Guide des archives: Aube.* Troyes, 1967.

Biraben, J.-H. *Les Hommes et la peste en France*, vol. 1. Paris and the Hague, 1975.

Birrell, J. "Peasant Craftsmen in the Medieval Forest." *Agricultural History Review* 17 (1969): 91–107.

Bisson, T. "The Problem of Feudal Monarchy: Aragon, Catalonia, and France." *Speculum* 53 (1978): 460–78.

Bitton, F. *Histoire de la ville de Sens.* 1943.

Black Names in America: Origins and Usage. Compiled by N. Puckett. Edited by M. Heller. Boston, 1975.

Blaise, A. *Lexicon latinitatis medii aevi.* Tournholt, 1975.

Blin, L. "Recherches sur un chemin médiéval de l'Yonne à la Loire." SHYonne *Bulletin* 108 (1976): 17–39.

Bloch, M. *Feudal Society.* 2 vols. Translated by L. Manyon. Chicago, 1964.

———. *French Rural History.* Translated by J. Sondheimer. Berkeley and Los Angeles, 1966.

———. "Liberté et servitude personelles au moyen-âge." In *Mélanges historiques.* 1963.

———. *Rois et serfs.* 1920.

———. "Un Problème d'histoire comparée: La Ministérialité en France et en Allemagne." In *Mélanges historiques.* 1963.

Blondel, P. "La Vérité sur les chartes de fondation de l'abbaye de Saint-Pierre-le-Vif." SASens *Bulletin* 18 (1897): 183–216.

Bonneau, G. "Répertoire historique, archéologique, biographique indiquant par communes les articles . . . publiés dans les Bulletins, . . . Almanachs et Revues de l'Yonne." SHYonne *Bulletin* 84 (1930): 199–283.

Boswell, J. "*Expositio* and *Oblatio*: The Abandonment of Children and the Ancient and Medieval Family." *American Historical Review* 89 (1984): 10–33.

Bouvier, H. *Histoire de l'Eglise et de l'ancien archidiocèse de Sens.* 3 vols. Paris and Sens, 1906–11.

———. "Histoire de Saint-Pierre-le-Vif." SHYonne *Bulletin* 45 (1891): 5–212.

Bowers, R. "From Rolls to Riches: King's Clerks and Moneylending in Thirteenth-Century England." *Speculum* 58 (1983): 60–71.

Bowness, C. *Romany Magic.* Wellingborough, 1973.

Brissaud, J.-B. *A History of French Public Law.* Translated by J. Garner. Boston, 1915.

Brissot. "Notice sur Villeneuve-le-Roi." SASens *Bulletin* 10 (1872): 129–45.

Britton, E. *The Community of the Vill.* Toronto, 1977.

Brown, E. "The Tyranny of a Construct: Feudalism and Historians of

Medieval Europe." *American Historical Review* 79 (1974): 1063–88.

Brullée, L. "Notice sur l'ancienne abbaye de Notre-Dame de La Pommeraye." SASens *Bulletin* 2 (1851): 82–111.

Burrows, T. "Unmaking 'the Middle Ages,'" *Journal of Medieval History* 7 (1981): 127–34.

Buzy, J. "Etude historique et littéraire sur Sainte-Théodéchilde." SASens *Bulletin* 10 (1872): 197–209.

Cailleaux, D. "Histoire du monastère Notre-Dame des Célestins de Sens." SASens *Bulletin*, 1975, pp. 12–21.

Carlier, A. "Le Popelin de Sens." SASens *Bulletin* 7 (1861): 54–67.

Carré, G. "Voies romaines dans l'arrondissement de Sens." SASens *Bulletin* 8 (1863): 1–15.

Carrez, H. "Noms de personne féminins dans la région dijonnaise." *Annales de Bourgogne* 14 (1942): 85–129.

Challe, A. "Les Chroniquers sénonais du moyen-âge." SHYonne *Bulletin* 35 (1881): 77–90.

Chandenier, F. *Le P. Laire, la Bibliothèque et le Musée de la ville de Sens.* Sens, 1900.

Chartraire, E. "Les Prisons de l'Officialité de Sens en l'an 1331." SASens *Bulletin* 30 (1916): 99–125.

Chastel, G. *Sainte-Colombe de Sens.* Niort, 1939.

Cipolla, C. *Before the Industrial Revolution.* 2d ed. New York and London, 1980.

Cohen, E. "Patterns of Crime in Fourteenth-Century Paris." *French Historical Studies* 11 (1980): 307–27.

Cousin, P. "Anciens ermites et ermitages de l'actuel diocèse de Sens," parts 1, 2. SHYonne *Bulletin* 101 (1965–66): 81–165; 102 (1967–68): 5–106.

Cutler, S. *The Law of Treason and Treason Trials in Later Medieval France.* Cambridge, 1981.

Dauphin, J.-L. "La Vallée de Valprofonde et la naissance de Villeneuve-sur-Yonne," part 1. SHYonne *Bulletin* 108 (1976): 5–16.

Defer, E.-E. "Histoire de Traînel." SAAube *Mémoires* 48 (1884): 121–369.

Dégouvenain, L. "Des Chartes de commune et d'affranchissement." Société d'Etudes d'Avallon *Bulletin*, 1862, pp. 54–112.

Delaborde, H.-F. *Jean de Joinville et les seigneurs de Joinville.* 1894.

Delisle, L. "Les Opérations financières des Templiers." *Mémoires de l'Académie des Inscriptions et Belles-lettres* 33 (1889): 1–248.

Denisova-Khatchaturian, N. "Sotsial'no-politicheskie aspekty nachal'noi istorii general'nikh shtatov vo Frantsii." In *Evropa v srednie veka.* Moscow, 1972.

De Roover, R. *Money, Banking and Credit in Medieval Bruges*. Cambridge, Mass., 1948.

DeWindt, E. *Land and People in Holywell-cum-Needingworth*. Toronto, 1972.

Dictionary of the Middle Ages. 5 vols. to date. New York, 1982–.

Dictionnaire de biographie française. 15 vols. to date. 1929–.

Dictionnaire topographique de la France: Aube. Edited by T. Boutiot and E. Socard. 1874.

———. *Seine-et-Marne*. Edited by H. Stein and J. Hubert. 1954.

———. *Yonne*. Edited by M. Quantin. 1872.

Dion, R. *Histoire de la vigne et du vin en France*. 1959.

Dockès, P. *Medieval Slavery and Liberation*. Translated by A. Goldhammer. Chicago, 1982.

Doehaerd, R. "Un Paradoxe géographique: Laon, capitale du vin." *Annales: ESC* 5 (1950): 145–65.

Duby, G. "The Diffusion of Cultural Patterns in Feudal Society." *Past and Present*, no. 39 (1968): 3–10.

———. "Medieval Agriculture, 900–1500." In *Fontana Economic History of Europe*, vol. 1, *The Middle Ages*, edited by C. Cipolla. London, 1972.

———. *Rural Economy and Country Life in the Medieval West*. Translated by C. Postan. London, 1968.

Duplès-Agier, H. "Notice sur une pièce trouvée au Trésor des Chartes et concernant la ville de Sens au XIIIe siècle." *SASens Bulletin* 2 (1851): 57–69.

Dyer, C. *Lords and Peasants in a Changing Society: The Estates of the Bishopric of Worcester, 680–1540*. Cambridge, 1980.

Eberhard, W., and F. Seibt, eds. *Europa 1400: Die Krise des Spätmittelalters*. Stuttgart, 1984.

English, B. *The Lords of Holderness, 1086–1260*. Oxford, 1979.

Evergates, T. *Feudal Society in the Bailliage of Troyes*. Baltimore, 1975.

Fesler, J. "French Field Administration: The Beginnings." *Comparative Studies in Society and History* 5 (1962–63): 76–111.

Filloux, R. "Week-end templier dans l'Yonne, 10–11 juin 1972." *Cahiers du Temple*, 1973, pp. 25–29.

Fossier, R. "Land, Castle, Money and Family in the Formation of the Seigneuries." In *Medieval Settlement*, edited by P. Sawyer. London, 1976.

———. *La Terre et les hommes en Picardie*. 2 vols. 1968.

Fournier, P. *Les Officialités au moyen-âge*. 1880.

Fourquin, G. *Lordship and Feudalism*. London, 1976.

Fourrey, R. *Sens, ville d'art et d'histoire.* Lyon, 1953.

Francis, A. *The Wine Trade.* London, 1972.

Gams, P. *Series episcoporum ecclesiae catholicae.* Graz, 1957.

Geremek, B. *Les Marginaux parisiens aux XIVe et XVe siècles.* 1976.

Godefroy, F. *Lexique de l'ancien français.* Rev. ed. 1901.

Grayzel, S. *The Church and the Jews in the Thirteenth Century.* Philadelphia, 1933.

Guérin, P. "Enquête faite par le chantre de Senlis et le bailli de Sens." SASens *Bulletin* 13 (1885).

———. "Les Monuments préhistoriques dans la région de l'Yonne." SHYonne *Bulletin* 87 (1933).

Hallam, H. "The Climate of Eastern England 1250–1350." *Agricultural History Review* 32 (1984): 124–32.

Harvey, B. *Westminster Abbey and Its Estates in the Middle Ages.* Oxford, 1977.

Hatcher, J. "English Serfdom and Villeinage: Towards a Reassessment." *Past and Present*, no. 90 (1981): 3–39.

Haucour, L. d'. *Histoire de la ville de Sens.* 1911.

Henneman, J. *Royal Taxation in Fourteenth Century France.* Princeton, 1971.

Hilton, R. *Bond Men Made Free: Medieval Peasant Movements and the English Rising of 1381.* London, 1973.

———. *The Decline of Serfdom in Medieval England.* London and Elsewhere, 1969.

———. *The English Peasantry in the Later Middle Ages.* Oxford, 1975.

———. "Towns in English Feudal Society." *Review* 3 (1979): 3–20.

Histoire de la France rurale. 4 vols. 1975–1976.

Hockey, S. *Quarr Abbey and Its Lands 1132–1631.* Leicester, 1970.

Hohl, C. *Guide des Archives de l'Yonne.* Auxerre, 1974.

Horson, P.-V. *Recherches historiques sur Pont-sur-Yonne.* Sens, 1878.

Howell, M. "The Late Medieval and Early Modern City." *Trends in History* 2 (1981): 5–18.

Hubert, J. "La Frontière occidentale du comté de Champagne." In *Recueil de travaux offert à M. Clovis Brunel.* 1955.

Hugues, A. *Les Routes de Seine-et-Marne avant 1789.* Melun, 1897.

Hure, A. *Les Ciments à tuileau romain et post-romain . . . de Sens et de l'ensemble de l'Yonne.* Auxerre, 1935.

———. "Les Silos de Michery (Yonne)." SHYonne *Bulletin* 68 (1914): 151–58.

Huyghebaert, N. *Les Documents nécrologiques.* Tournholt, 1972.

Hyams, P. *King, Lords and Peasants in Medieval England.* Oxford, 1980.

Jones, A. "Harvest Customs and Labourers' Perquisites in Southern England, 1150–1350: The Corn Harvest." *Agricultural History Review* 25 (1977): 14–22.

———. "Harvest Customs and Labourers' Perquisites in Southern England, 1150–1350: The Hay Harvest." *Agricultural History Review* 25 (1977): 98–107.

———. "Land Measurement in England, 1150–1350." *Agricultural History Review* 27 (1979): 10–18.

Jordan, W. "An Aspect of Credit in Picardy in the 1240s: The Deterioration of Jewish-Christian Financial Relations." *Revue des Etudes juives* 142 (1983): 141–52.

———. "Bailli." *Dictionary of the Middle Ages* 2:52–53.

———. "The Cistercian Nunnery of La Cour Notre-Dame de Michery: A House that Failed," *Revue bénédictine* 101 (1986): 165–76.

———. "Communal Administration in France, 1257–1270." *Revue belge de philologie et d'histoire* 59 (1981): 292–313.

———. "Corvée." *Dictionary of the Middle Ages* 3:612–13.

———. "Jewish-Christian Relations in Mid-Thirteenth Century France: An Unpublished *Enquête* from Picardy." *Revue des Etudes juives* 138 (1979): 47–55.

———. *Louis IX and the Challenge of the Crusade.* Princeton, 1979.

———. "Mainmort." *Dictionary of the Middle Ages.* Forthcoming.

———. "Mortmain." *Dictionary of the Middle Ages.* Forthcoming.

Julliot, G. "Notices anonymes sur le rû de Mondereau." SASens *Bulletin* 11 (1877): 184–204.

Kaeuper, R. *Bankers to the Crown: The Riccardi of Lucca and Edward I.* Princeton, 1973.

King, E. *Peterborough Abbey, 1086–1310: A Study in the Land Market.* Cambridge, 1973.

Knackstedt, W. *Moskau: Studien zur Geschichte einer mittelalterlichen Stadt.* Wiesbaden, 1975.

Kosminsky, E. *Studies in the Agrarian History of England in the Thirteenth Century.* Edited by R. Hilton. Translated by R. Kisch. Oxford, 1956.

Lajon, N. "Sur les menhirs de La Postolle." SHYonne *Bulletin* 86 (1932): 239–42.

Laperouse, G. "Rapport sur les monuments primitifs (dolmens et menhirs) de l'arrondissement de Nogent-sur-Seine." SAAube *Mémoires* 28 (1864): 93–123.

Larcher de Lavernade, C. *Histoire de la ville de Sens.* Sens, 1845.

Laurent, J. "Le Bailliage de Sens du XIIIe au XVIIIe s." *Revue des questions historiques* 113 (1930): 319–49.

Lecoy de La Marche, A. "Les Coutumes et péages de Sens." *Bibliothèque de l'Ecole de Chartes* 27 (1866): 265–300.

Lehoux, F. *Le Bourg Saint-Germain-des-Près.* 1951.

Lemaître, J.-L. "Les Obituaires français." *Revue d'histoire de l'Eglise de France* 64 (1978): 69–81.

———. *Répertoire des documents nécrologiques français.* 2 vols. 1980.

Le Roy Ladurie, E. "Family and Inheritance in Sixteenth-Century France." In *Family and Inheritance: Rural Society in Western Europe, 1200–1800*, edited by J. Goody et al. Cambridge, 1976.

Lhuillier, T. "Inventaire de titres concernant la seigneurie que les religieuses de l'abbaye royale N.-D. du Lys, près Melun, possédaient à Mâlay-le-Roi." SASens *Bulletin* 10 (1872): 347–57.

McClure, P. "Patterns of Migration in the Late Middle Ages." *Economic History Review* 32 (1979): 167–82.

———. "Surnames from English Placenames as Evidence for Mobility in the Middle Ages." *Local Historian* 13 (1978): 80–86.

Maillard, C., and C. Berruyer. "Les Rapports entre archevêques et monastères dans l'archidiaconé de Sens." *Bulletin philologique et historique*, 1979, pp. 121–35.

Mate, M. "Property Investment by Canterbury Cathedral Priory 1250–1400." *Journal of British Studies* 23 (1984): 1–21.

Mignardot, M. "Monographie de Michery: Ière partie." *Société archéologique et culturelle de Pont sur Yonne*, no. 2 (1965–66): 55–81.

Moiset, C. "Essai sur l'origine des noms et prénoms en France et particulièrement dans la région de l'Yonne." SHYonne *Bulletin* 47 (1893): 33–50.

———. "Les Usages, croyances, traditions, superstitions, etc. avant existé autrefois ou existant encore dans les divers pays du département de l'Yonne." SHYonne *Bulletin* 42 (1888): 5–157.

Mollat, M., and P. Wolff. *The Popular Revolutions of the Late Middle Ages.* Translated by A. Lytton-Sells. London, 1973.

Monceaux, H. "Les Coutumes et péages de la vicomté de Sens." SHYonne *Bulletin* 34 (1880): 303–48.

Moreau, H. "Les Loups dans l'Yonne." SHYonne *Bulletin* 112 (1980): 177–91.

New Catholic Encyclopedia. 15 vols. New York, 1967.

Nicholas, D. "Patterns of Social Mobility." In *One Thousand Years: Western Europe in the Middle Ages*, edited by R. Demolen. Boston, 1974.

Notice historique sur la construction de la cathédrale de Sens. N.p., n.d. (AD: Yonne, Salle de Lecteur no. 1128 F 1).

Patault, A.-M. *Hommes et femmes de corps en Champagne méridionale à la fin du moyen-âge*. Saint-Nicolas-de-Port, 1978.

Paustian, P. "The Evolution of Personal Naming Practices Among American Blacks." *Names* 26 (1978): 177–91.

Perrin, J. "Histoire d'un cours d'eau: Le Rû de Gravereau." SASens *Bulletin* 28 (1913): 1–154.

———. "Le Rû Mondereau: Etude complémentaire." SASens *Bulletin* 38 (1931–33): 189–236.

Pignaud-Péguet, M. *Histoire illustrée des départements: Yonne*. 1913.

Pirenne, H. *Economic and Social History of Medieval Europe*. Translated by I. Clegg. New York, 1937.

Pissier, A. "L'Abbaye Notre-Dame de Dilo au diocèse de Sens." SHYonne *Bulletin* 82 (1928): 31–148.

———. "Etudes historiques sur Dixmont." SHYonne *Bulletin* 61 (1907): 3–124, 217–90.

———. "Les Frontières de l'Ile-de-France et de la Champagne du XIIe au XIVe siècle." SASens *Bulletin* 40 (1937–38): 105–15.

Pollock, F., and F. Maitland. *The History of English Law Before the Time of Edward I*. 2 vols. 2d ed. Cambridge, 1968.

Porée, C. "Catalogue des chartes de franchises des communautés d'habitants de l'Yonne." SHYonne *Bulletin* 84 (1930): 165–97.

———. *Histoire des rues et des maisons de Sens*. Sens, 1920.

Postan, M. *The Medieval Economy and Society*. London, 1972.

Prou, M. *Les Coutumes de Lorris*. 1884.

———. "Etudes sur les chartes de fondation de l'abbaye de Saint-Pierre-le-Vif." SASens *Bulletin* 17 (1895): 40–89 (second pagination).

———. *Fouillés opérées à Sens, sur l'emplacement de l'ancienne église de Saint-Pierre-le-Vif*. Nogent-le-Rotrou, 1895.

Prütz, H. "Die finanziellen Operationen der Hospitaliter." *Sitzungsberichte der bayerische Akademie, Philosophisch-Historisch Classe*, 1906.

Pugh, R. *Imprisonment in Medieval England*. Cambridge, 1968.

Quantin, M. *Histoire de la commune de Sens*. Auxerre, 1857.

———. "Histoire de la rivière d'Yonne." SHYonne *Bulletin* 39 (1885): 349–498.

———. "Histoire des ordres réligieux et militaires du Temple et de Saint-Jean de Jerusalem dans le département de l'Yonne." *Annuaire de l'Yonne*, 1882.

———. *Inventaire-sommaire des archives communales: Sens*. Sens, 1870.

———. *Inventaire-sommaire des archives départementales: Yonne*.

Série G. Auxerre, 1873.

Série H. Auxerre, 1882.

Séries A–F. Auxerre, 1868.

———. "Recherches sur le tiers-état au moyen-âge dans les pays qui forment aujourd'hui le département de l'Yonne." SHYonne *Bulletin* 5 (1851).

Quantin, M., and Boucheron. "Mémoire sur les voies romaines qui traversent le département de l'Yonne." SHYonne *Bulletin* 18 (1864): 5–72.

Quesvers, P. *Note sur quelques paroisses de l'ancien diocèse de Sens*. Sens, 1893.

Raban, S. *The Estates of Thorney and Crowland: A Study in Medieval Monastic Land Tenure*. Department of Land Economy, Cambridge University, Occasional Paper no. 7, 1977.

———. *Mortmain Legislation and the English Church*. Cambridge, 1982.

Raftis, J. *The Estates of Ramsey Abbey*. Toronto, 1957.

———. *Tenure and Mobility: Studies in the Social History of the Medieval English Village*. Toronto, 1964.

———. *Warboys: Two Hundred Years in the Life of an English Mediaeval Village*. Toronto, 1974.

Razi, Z. *Life, Marriage and Death in a Medieval Parish: Economy, Society and Demography in Halesowen*. Cambridge, 1980.

———. "The Struggles Between the Abbots of Halesowen and their Tenants in the Thirteenth and Fourteenth Centuries." In *Social Relations and Ideas*, edited by T. Aston et al. Cambridge, 1983.

———. "The Toronto School's Reconstitution of Medieval Peasant Society: A Critical View." *Past and Present*, no. 85 (1979): 141–57.

Recueil des statuts, ordonnances et règlements synodaux de l'archidiocèse de Sens. Sens, 1854.

Régnier, E. "Histoire de l'abbaye des Escharlis." SHYonne *Bulletin* 67 (1913): 221–346.

Reyerson, K. "Changes in Testamentary Practice at Montpellier on the Eve of the Black Death." *Church History* 47 (1978): 253–69.

Richard, J. *Les Ducs de Bourgogne et la formation du Duché du XIe au XIVe siècle*. 1954.

Rocher, J.-P. "Bibliographie critique de l'histoire de la vigne dans l'Auxerrois." SHYonne *Bulletin* 103 (1969–70): 23–44.

Roy, M. "Le Couvent des Dominicains de Sens." SASens *Bulletin* 20 (1903): 99–221.

Saint-Jacob, P. de. *Les Paysans de la Bourgogne du nord au dernier siècle de l'ancien régime*. 1960.

Salomon. "Histoire de l'abbaye des Escharlis." SHYonne *Bulletin* 6 (1852): 387–450.

Sassier, Y. *Recherches sur le pouvoir comtal, en Auxerrois du Xe au début du XIIIe siècle.* Auxerre, 1980.

Sayles, G. *The Medieval Foundations of England.* New York, 1961.

Schramm, P. *Der König von Frankreich.* 2 vols. Weimar, 1939.

Sivéry, G. *L'Economie du royaume de France au siècle de saint Louis.* Lille, 1984.

————. "Mouvements de capitaux et taux d'intérêt en Occident au XIIIe siècle." *Annales: ESC,* 1983, pp. 137–50.

————. *Saint Louis et son siècle.* 1983.

————. *Structures agraires et vie rurale dans le Hainault à la fin du moyen-âge.* 2 vols. Lille, 1977–80.

Smith, R. "Some Thoughts on 'Hereditary' and 'Proprietary' Rights in Land Under Customary Law in Thirteenth and Fourteenth Century England." *Law and History Review* 1 (1983): 95–128.

Southern, R. *The Making of the Middle Ages.* New Haven, 1953.

Strayer, J. "Economic Conditions in the County of Beaumont-le-Roger." *Speculum* 26 (1951): 277–87.

Tierney, B., ed. *The Middle Ages.* Vol. 2, *Readings in Medieval History.* New York, 1974.

Titow, J. *English Rural Society, 1200–1350.* London, 1969.

Tomasson, R. "The Continuity of Icelandic Names and Naming Patterns." *Names* 23 (1975): 281–89.

"Toponomastique de la région de Sens." SASens *Bulletin* 42 (n.d.).

Tuchman, B. *A Distant Mirror: The Calamitous Fourteenth Century.* New York, 1978.

Turlan, J. *La Commune et le corps de ville de Sens.* 1942.

Vajon, E. *Monographie de la commune d'Evry.* Sens, 1914.

Valous, G. de. *Le Temporel et la situation financière des établissements de l'ordre de Cluny du XIIIe au XIVe siècle.* Liguge, 1935.

Wormsley, W. "Tradition and Change in Imbonggu Names and Naming Practices." *Names* 28 (1980): 183–94.

Yver, J. *Egalité entre héritiers et exclusion des enfants dotés.* 1966.

Index

143

The Middle Ages
Edward Peters, General Editor

Christian Society and the Crusades, 1198–1229. Sources in Translation, including The Capture of Damietta by Oliver of Paderborn. Edited by Edward Peters

The First Crusade: The Chronicle of Fulcher of Chartres and Other Source Materials. Edited by Edward Peters

Love in Twelfth-Century France. John C. Moore

The Burgundian Code: The Book of Constitutions or Law of Gundobad and Additional Enactments. Translated by Katherine Fischer Drew

The Lombard Laws. Translated, with an Introduction, by Katherine Fischer Drew

From St. Francis to Dante: Translations from the Chronicle of the Franciscan Salimbene (1221–1288). G. G. Coulton

The Duel and the Oath. Parts I and II of Superstition and Force. Henry Charles Lea. Introduction by Edward Peters

The Ordeal. Part III of Superstition and Force. Henry Charles Lea

Torture. Part IV of Superstition and Force. Henry Charles Lea

Witchcraft in Europe, 1110–1700: A Documentary History. Edited by Alan C. Kors and Edward Peters

The Scientific Achievement of the Middle Ages. Richard C. Dales

History of the Lombards. Paul the Deacon. Translated by William Dudley Foulke